# START & RUN AN ART TEACHING BUSINESS

# START & RUN AN ART
# TEACHING BUSINESS

## Tanya Freedman

**Self-Counsel Press**
*(a division of)*
International Self-Counsel Press Ltd.
USA    Canada

*Self-Counsel Press acknowledges the financial support of the Government of Canada through the Book Publishing Industry Development Program (*BPIDP*) for our publishing activities.*

*Printed in Canada.*

*First edition: 2007*


**Library and Archives Canada Cataloguing in Publication**

Freedman, Tanya, 1963–
    Start and run an art teaching business / Tanya Freedman.

(Self-counsel business series)
Includes bibliographical references.
ISBN 978-1-55180-734-8


    1. Art schools—Management.  2. New business enterprises.
I. Title.  II. Series.


N325.F74 2007          707.1          C2007-901978-1

*The paintings* Rose, Water Lilies, *and* Sunflower *used as illustrations throughout the book are by the author.*

**ANCIENT FOREST FRIENDLY** Self-Counsel Press is committed to protecting the environment and to the responsible use of natural resources. We are acting on this commitment by working with suppliers and printers to phase out our use of paper produced from ancient forests. This book is one step toward that goal. It is printed on 100 percent ancient-forest-free paper (100 percent post-consumer recycled), processed chlorine- and acid-free.


**Self-Counsel Press**
*(a division of)*
International Self-Counsel Press Ltd.

1704 North State Street          1481 Charlotte Road
Bellingham, WA  98225           North Vancouver, BC  V7J 1H1
USA                                     Canada

# CONTENTS

## 4  CLASS PRICES AND MATERIALS                          67

## 5  YOUR BUSINESS PLAN                                   73

## 11   GROWING YOUR BUSINESS

## APPENDIX

# EXERCISES

# FORMS

# SAMPLES

# NOTICE TO READERS

The author, the publisher, and the vendor of this book make no representations or warranties regarding the outcome or the use to which the information in this book is put and are not assuming any liability for any claims, losses, or damages arising out of the use of this book. The reader should not rely on the author or publisher of this book for any professional advice.

Prices, commissions, fees, and other costs mentioned in the text or shown in samples in this book probably do not reflect real costs where you live. Inflation and other factors, including geography, can cause the costs you might encounter to be much higher or even much lower than those we show. The dollar amounts shown are simply intended as representative examples.

# FOREWORD

The role of mentor is an extremely important one, providing guidance, counseling, coaching, and professional advice learned through experience. Effective mentors share not only what they know, and who they know, but also who they are. In *Start & Run an Art Teaching Business*, Tanya Freedman, my protégée and friend, acts as a mentor to her readers.

For Tanya, being successful isn't just about believing in herself and her talents, it is also about reaching out and connecting with others who are willing to help her succeed. Tanya has built on her extensive networking skills and business acumen to accomplish exactly what she set out to do: make this a must-read book.

*Start & Run an Art Teaching Business* is a template for anyone who wants to succeed in the business of teaching art. Allow Tanya to guide you through the planning and infancy of your new business. Your dreams can come true if you learn from an expert.

*Donna Messer*

DIRECTOR OF CONNECTUS
COMMUNICATIONS CANADA

# ACKNOWLEDGMENTS

Huge thanks to everyone at Self-Counsel Press for making this book the best it can be — especially to Richard Day and Barbara Kuhne for your receptiveness to my ideas, and to my enthusiastic and detail-oriented editors, Tanya Howe and Grace Yaginuma, who made revisions seem like fun and not at all like work. I appreciate your wisdom and patience, as well as all the help from the marketing and production teams for teaching me so much.

Thanks to my friends, old and new, for always supporting me in my business and writing endeavors and throughout my life. Thank you to Donna Messer, my networking guru, mentor, and friend. Thanks to Traci Tomkin, Heather Skoll, Adine Owieczka, and Anne and Jose Mulackal. I extend my thanks to members of the Jolly Great Writer's Group, the Golden Gavel Toastmasters, and pals from TRW, as well as Ian Kennedy, Mary Lou di Paolo, Barry Moore, and Patricia Ruhl, copywriter and ambassador extraordinaire.

Special gratitude goes out to all my Jolly Good Art students, young and young at heart, and to all the parents who have provided amazing feedback and support. You have made me believe that my artistic passions have touched and inspired creativity in more lives than I could have ever imagined. I owe much to my very first art teacher, Miss Dray, whose encouragement has always stayed with me. And thank you, Mum, for saying, "You can do anything you put your mind to."

I appreciate the kindness of my neighbors and true friends: Anne Arbour, Elsa, Ellen, Michelle, Pablo, and Lynda and Gary Freedman. Thank you so much for being there, especially in the past year when my family and I needed you most.

Finally, I thank the two loves of my life, Austin and Natalia, for your unconditional faith and for constantly bringing energy, humor, and happiness into my life. You remind me of what life is all about.

# INTRODUCTION

It is a well-known fact that children's learning and development potential improves significantly when they are stimulated by arts programs. Yet many schools are eliminating programs such as art and music because of funding cutbacks. After-school art programs are increasingly in demand as parents actively seek to cultivate as many of their children's talents as possible.

And it is not just children who can benefit from art classes. Adults, too, are seeking a creative outlet, especially as the effects of stress reach epidemic proportions.

More and more people are using their creative talents to pursue alternative careers and becoming entrepreneurs in the field of art, crafts, music, and dance. Even some of the lost crafts such as knitting, sewing, and crocheting are being set up as new business ventures.

In this book I share with you my own experiences of opening my school, Jolly Good Art. This book is a blueprint to help you craft your own business using your unique artistic talents. What art school do you dream of starting? This is an exciting new venture, and in addition to having a genuine love and passion for creating and teaching art, you must remain motivated and excited at every stage. Let this book be the companion that motivates you as you start and run your enterprise. It will take your art school business from conception to profitable reality — and beyond.

If you are new to the world of business, I highly recommend that you complete all the exercises. They are intended to help you with all the brainstorming you must do, especially when it comes to charting realistic short- and long-term goals. You will get a better idea of where to start, how to cultivate your own abilities, and how to nurture your students' creativity and talents. And the practical advice about time management should help you become more organized and therefore accomplish even more. Time is a more precious commodity than most people admit or realize!

Whether you are a new or an experienced entrepreneur, I hope the ideas in this book will spark your imagination in an exciting new direction, and help you become an even better communicator, teacher, and networker. I'm also here to remind you that your expectations at the outset should be grounded and realistic. Be honest with yourself and others, and cultivate your integrity as a respected businessperson. When it comes to operating your business, sometimes there is no right or wrong, only what you learn along the way.

This book also comes with a CD-ROM. There are extensive lists of resources, including websites and organizations.

Make wise choices, and make the most of your life now! I trust you have unique talents and visions, and this book is here to help you start a business doing something you enjoy. I wish you the greatest joy in discovering your fullest potential and then living it.

# GETTING YOUR BUSINESS STARTED

*I don't care how much power, brilliance, or energy you have, if you don't harness it and focus it on a specific target and hold it there you're never going to accomplish as much as your ability warrants.*

— ZIG ZIGLAR

## The Conception of Jolly Good Art

My first business involved importing English antique furniture. Because of my love of antiques, and my knowledge of good quality furniture, it seemed a natural path to follow. I enjoyed what I did, but after three years of frequent traveling, my family obligations overtook the burgeoning success of my company.

I took a long, hard look at what it was I really wanted to do that would not end up compromising my marriage or motherhood. My husband and I analyzed my options. What did I really want to do and what could I do that wouldn't necessitate traveling? The

answer was art. I loved art, and an opportunity, by way of invitation to demonstrate my watercolor skills at a local ladies' social group, planted the seed of the Jolly Good Art Studio and School.

I wrote down a tentative plan for what I needed to do to earn a minimum monthly income. Rather than pressuring myself to start big, which would have made me feel overwhelmed, I decided to ease my way into the new venture. I researched and talked to people who I thought could give me advice. I talked to my friends with entrepreneurial backgrounds and the parents of my daughter's friends. I contacted other artists and anyone I respected to give me their honest opinions.

I began with small classes of four or five students, in after-school programs in my own home-based studio in my basement as well as off-site. I calculated the earnings potential and seriously considered what I wanted to achieve. Would it be worth it?

My mathematical equation was a basic one:

> Number of children x fee per child per month – costs (e.g., supplies, rent, and eventually staff) = monthly profit

Within a few months, using my marketing and networking skills, I took my home business to the next level. Registering my sole-ownership name of Jolly Good Art and insuring for maximum liability, I started with small classes for children and for stay-at-home or self-employed parents.

Before long I was also running various after-school (and after-work) and weekend programs in my home studio. The classes included painting and glass painting workshops for adults and weekend art classes for children of different ages and experience levels.

During that time, a parent of one of my students had asked me if I offered summer camp programs. It was March so I thought, "Why not?" It seemed right to expand my business. I took the initiative to plan and prepare a unique summer camp program. I had plenty of committed campers interested in joining and could therefore cover the costs of additional staff.

The last day of camp coincided with a seven-year-old boy's birthday. With a little extra planning, having selected special balloons and games to celebrate the official end of summer as well as his special day, the celebration was a success, and I was complimented for being able to organize such an event. Everyone could see I was a skilled professional. Could I organize another birthday party for the younger sibling, too? From there I added custom birthday parties to my menu of programs.

## Creative Visualization

If you are ready to conceptualize your business from an exciting idea to a living, breathing enterprise, start by using creative visualization. Some call it affirmation, while others see it as becoming attuned to the collective unconscious in which we are all connected to one another somehow.

Although I did not realize that what I was doing was called "creative visualization," I found this exercise to be of immense benefit while I was starting my business. It gave me the certainty and courage to forge ahead.

Going hand in hand with goal setting, Exercise 1 will assist you in forming a clearer picture of your future. (All the exercises in this book are also contained in the CD-ROM accompanying this book.) Beyond writing down goals that may at the beginning be uncertain, creative visualization can help you see deeply into your new future.

You may be skeptical and view this as a waste of your precious time, or you may see this as a chance for meditation. Think of it as creating your ideal painting on a virgin canvas, as opening yourself up to a realm of new possibilities. This exercise should only take you half an hour to an hour. At the price of some of your time and effort you may gain peace of mind and fire yourself up

# EXERCISE 1
# CREATIVE VISUALIZATION

For this exercise you will need a quiet place, a pen or pencil, and paper.

Go somewhere where there will be no interruptions or distractions (e.g., music or background sounds) for half an hour to an hour. Make sure your spot is away from people. For example, you could take a bubble bath or go to your garden or bedroom. You might also want to turn off your telephone ringer.

Now close your eyes and completely relax. Think about every part of your body relaxing from head to toe. It may take a while (e.g., 15 to 20 minutes) before you can totally relax and find the silence within you. Be patient and pay attention to your breathing, and the calming of your body and mind.

Now let your imagination soar and allow visions to enter your psyche. Imagine where you would like to be in your business in a few months, one year, three years, and five years. Stay with it, keeping your thoughts flowing in a constant positive direction. Block out any negative or critical thoughts. Also ignore anything negative or critical that other people may have said to you about your plans and ideas.

Reach for your pen and paper only when you are absolutely ready to leave the futurist world without losing the amazing images. Capture the whole dream in words — all the ideas, no matter how far-fetched they may seem — and write a date on the document. No one else needs to see the notes about your creative visualization exercise, so be as creative and wacky as your mind will allow.

You can choose to file this document away and revisit it in a few years or reread it often. Doing this exercise and saving it in writing will serve a greater purpose than you may first imagine.

to achieve those dreams. Behind every successful business, there's a tenacious entrepreneur who did not quit or give up on his or her vision.

## Setting goals

In order to get to the place you strive toward, you have to set realistic and achievable goals and write them down. This makes them real and tangible. Your action list should include only those actions that take you a step closer to your goals. Eliminate everything else. Stay on track and avoid being diverted from your goals, being distracted, or making excuses.

I experienced a great sense of accomplishment when I came across a list of goals I had prepared in my business school years. Despite the fact that some of the goals had seemed unattainable at the time, I was proud to see that I had achieved many of them. I was able to check off the following from my list:

- Found and run a successful art school

- Exhibit and sell my artwork internationally

- Be published in fiction and nonfiction

- Write how-to books

- Promote and teach business techniques

- Mentor others

- Participate in professional speaking forums and seminars

- Run workshops

- Interview people and be interviewed

Even though I had not referred to the long-forgotten list in years, the actual process of writing down the goals had engraved them into my psyche. But like everything in life, my list has evolved and has factored in the reality of juggling family and business life.

Years ago my ideal goals may have seemed unachievable, but within the first year or two of founding Jolly Good Art I was able to achieve many of them. So I know that far-fetched dreams can come true, but my current list of goals does take into account the reality of my life, priorities, and choices.

When you are setting your goals, include enough details to show you a clear way forward, who your market and target audience is, and a reasonable time line. Exercise 2 will help you with this.

## Identifying Your Experiences and Transferable Skills

"If you fail to prepare, prepare to fail." This adage stresses the importance of laying the strongest foundation possible for your business idea so it can develop into reality and succeed despite all the odds.

Conceptualizing, conducting market research, and preparing a business plan go together. You are preparing a canvas or a clod of clay. You are projecting a vision in your mind, and planning what you want to achieve in the short and long term. An artist may start with a small idea that grows into a series of artwork, or an inspired sketch that results in a wall-to-wall masterpiece. You are cutting your teeth, making the most

# EXERCISE 2
# SETTING YOUR GOALS

No matter how unrealistic or out of reach your goals may appear, write down as many goals as you would like to achieve over the next few weeks, months, and years. Be specific and set realistic dates for completing each projected task.

Date: _____

| Goal | Subtasks | Time frame/Projected completion date |
|------|----------|--------------------------------------|
| 1.   | a)       |                                      |
|      | b)       |                                      |
|      | c)       |                                      |
| 2.   | a)       |                                      |
|      | b)       |                                      |
|      | c)       |                                      |
| 3.   | a)       |                                      |
|      | b)       |                                      |
|      | c)       |                                      |

List all your responsibilities — including financial, personal, and family obligations — that may influence your business plans.

of your strengths and transferable skills, and feeling your way toward the start line. Be a sponge: Get exposed to different concepts and become inspired by those you admire. Be flexible and prepare to go with the flow of where your creativity and new ideas lead you.

Some people gain experience in their desired field of art before starting up their own art business. Some buy a business or franchise, or hatch a brand new business. Some either achieve moderate or fantastic success — or fold within the first three to five years. They may not have planned thoroughly, utilized all of their strengths, or enlisted expert help during the crucial start-up phase.

At the conception phase of Jolly Good Art I took the time to list my experiences and transferable skills. I was also determined to concentrate on what I absolutely loved to do.

Identifying your experiences and transferable skills is an important step to finding the area of business that you will excel at. For example, my friend Elizabeth began her business by teaching her children how to sew. Eventually parents of her children's friends were asking Elizabeth to teach their children. She now has six stores and is sponsored by a major sewing machine company.

What can you glean from your past and present? Which passions burn brightly? If you picked up this book and are anything like me, you probably get lots of inspiration from anything connected with art, such as TV programs, instructional videos, and books about the art masters. This is a significant clue that you might consider becoming an art teacher.

## How you can turn your creativity into a business

Self-expression through visual art and through the written word are my parallel loves. My own art career started when I opened myself up to new and uncharted territories. A local minister's wife loved my custom thank-you card, which I had produced from one of my original paintings, and she asked if I taught art. Could I do a watercolor demonstration at the next ladies' social? Absolutely. I prepared for it, got all the materials ready, and did my best. It was well received; I even inspired some of the ladies to return to their long-forgotten interest in creating art. (One of these ladies now sells her artwork nationally!)

Next, I was asked if I could run classes at the local community center. Through these community contacts my database of interested clients grew larger. That is how simply it started for me. Word spread, and my students' siblings, friends, and school classmates wanted to create their own artwork to be proud of. Within seven months of registering my business I seriously contemplated expanding to an even larger studio.

Being open to opportunities and suggestions, and trying something new outside of your comfort zone may pay dividends. Pay close attention to the situations in which you thrive. If you find yourself constantly returning to your passion for art or other creative activities connected to it, and this passion feeds your soul despite its lack of feasible profitability, then pay attention to what your subconscious is telling you. Maybe you have been told repeatedly to pursue a "real" career — to be professional and practical — when you spend hours of your time immersed in your art, experimenting and creating pieces everyone adores. Take serious stock of how you can combine your passion for art with the reality of earning a living. Find opportunities to start using your creativity to bring in money.

Exercise 3 will help you explore what you want to do creatively with your business.

Do you feel that you are not quite ready yet? You may think that you have too many responsibilities that prevent you from starting the ball rolling. Do not let your dreams wither, however. You can still plan for the medium and long term at your own manageable pace. This will give you time to absorb new ideas and help you elevate your comfort level while plodding through life's realities and earning a living at your regular day job. Your goals are in your hands. You have to be prepared to take great strides and climb up that rocky mountain of business success. No one will make it happen for you. Whether or not you achieve your goals depends on the extent to which you are willing to —

- delve into your psyche;
- capitalize on your strengths;
- sacrifice spare time — which means less time for watching TV, engaging in hobbies, and having a busy social life, especially at the beginning;
- learn to balance family and business time;
- face your shortfalls and improve on them;
- learn from others around you; and
- believe in yourself.

Exercise 4 will take you to the next stage of turning your vision into reality. Your answers to this exercise will help you gain insight into some important areas you will need to consider when conducting market research and creating your business plan, which is discussed in more detail in Chapters 5 and 6.

Having completed Exercise 4, where do your discoveries lead you? Are you hesitant, ready to forge ahead, or actually practicing some of these steps?

If you are hesitant and not quite sure where and how to start, consider doing business on a small scale. Combine forces with another business or start working with a partner. By reading this book you are on your way to starting your business. Pay attention to the exercises and advice in this book, talk to respected advisers, and network. Clarify in your mind the best place for starting your business.

Maybe you are ready and you know you have a good idea and great potential. As long as you have done your preliminary homework and are not going to start your business by trial and error with a "hope for the best" attitude, then go for it. If you have any reservations, however, take some more time to prepare yourself.

## Look, Listen, and Learn

Sometimes eager entrepreneurs may skip seemingly unimportant steps in the planning, marketing, and strategizing stages at the start. Mistakes are inevitable, but if we are equipped with the right knowledge, and we prioritize and remind ourselves to be patient, we are halfway down the road to success.

## EXERCISE 3
## CONCEPTUALIZING YOUR ART-RELATED BUSINESS

1.  Can you visualize yourself in your own art-related business? If so, describe your vision. If not, list the hurdles you see.

2.  Describe the ideal situation in which you would conduct your business.

3.  What would you ideally like to spend all your time doing if you didn't have money, time, or other constraints in your life right now?

4.  What have you got to lose by trying the above-mentioned activity?

5.  In your artwork, do you love a particular medium or do you like to explore all sorts of media (glass or silk painting, mosaics, clay, scrapbooking, etc.)? Are there any other lesser-known materials you enjoy working with?

6.  What would you ideally like to do with your particular artistic talents? Would you combine them with other skills or expertise? (Think outside the box. Be as quirky and free-spirited as you possibly can.)

7.  Can you foresee yourself doing this activity as a business venture in the future?

Research how others have gone about starting up their art schools and art businesses. Conceptualize your ideas and then start to achieve your goals by taking action.

## EXERCISE 4
# ARE YOU READY TO BEGIN?

1.  Will you be a sole teacher who starts out by teaching small classes?

2.  Will you employ the services of specialist teachers? When? How many?

3.  Are you prepared to supervise your staff and assistants?

4.  What are your personal time constraints? (For example, if you are a parent of small children, what contingency plans do you have for looking after your own children in the case of an emergency?)

5.  How much money will you need to start your business?

6.  How big do you want your business to be when you start?

7.  When do you plan to expand the business?

8.  Where do you plan to start the business (for example, in a studio outside your home or in your own residence)?

You may find that reading this book will prepare you for or confirm your ideas about your impending venture. I cannot overstate the importance of doing the preliminary homework and, if necessary, delaying your dream by a few months or even a year or two. Always keep your long-term success in focus. You are building a stronger foothold for your business to flourish and last. Adopt the sure and methodical approach of the tortoise over that of the erratic and risky hare. The latter may bring fast apparent success, but quickly leads to burnout.

No one but you can do the work of researching into what is right for you — not even your spouse or partner, unless you plan to work together. You know yourself better than anyone else, and I hope this book can help you gain more insight into starting and running a successful art teaching business, whether you plan to do it alone or with the support of others.

## Apprenticing or teaching, and continuing your education

Before starting out on your own, and depending on your confidence and experience, you may want to become a part-time or full-time apprentice or take a teaching job. There is no better way to learn the ropes than by witnessing trade secrets while working alongside other teachers or an art school owner.

You will become aware of how much work goes into all the programs and the smooth workings of a school, and the many hats an owner has to wear. You will see what types of pitfalls could be in store for you in your own enterprise later on. It may prove to be an invaluable experience.

And of course, you can go back to school yourself, as a student, if only to take a short course or workshop. Your local colleges, business resource centers, and libraries can provide you with a list of programs, whether they are business related, or related to theories of teaching and instruction. This is also a great way to form a social network.

## Learning from children

I have come up with the best ideas for projects, study subjects, and programs with the help of my young daughter. She taught me to listen intently to my students. As a teacher, you must encourage the vibrant freshness children possess and help them capture it in their art. Children are naturally curious; have them share and explore. Listen to them and learn from them. You may find that they invigorate your own creative spirit.

## Contacting other artists and entrepreneurs

Another way for you to connect is to contact artists and creative entrepreneurs to find out how they began. Research the backgrounds of artists and creative entrepreneurs that you respect most. Find out how they went about making and shaping their careers. If possible, contact some of these artists or entrepreneurs directly and ask them for advice. Create a list of questions to ask these people before you talk to them.

The best way to initiate contact is to email them your questions. Email eliminates geographical distance and time differences and gives people time to consider your questions, which means that they may answer the questions more thoroughly when you finally talk to them on the telephone.

Ask open-ended questions that will encourage your interviewees to trust you. If they are in a different state, province, or country, they probably won't see you as competition and you may be able to ask specific questions about their pricing and business strategies. Gauge their comfort level from the length and content of their replies.

Remember to always be professional. For example, if you ask for a certain amount of their time, keep your promise, and arrange another meeting or phone conversation if you need more time. After your interview is completed, thank them for their time with a personal note or by email. Keep the channels open and friendly. By the same token, remember to be there for other people who may approach you for your expertise later in your career.

## Home-Based Studio Versus Rented Studio

You will need to decide if your home is big enough for a home-based studio. If it is not, then you will need to consider renting space for a studio.

### Home-based studio

Using an area of your home (or maybe a building on your property) for your studio can have many benefits. For starters, you are in control of your own environment and have no one but your family to answer to about what goes on in your studio; for example, your students can smash tiles to make mosaics and not worry about being too loud when working on their art projects.

Another benefit is that you can have as few classes as you like without having to worry about the studio earning its keep, increasing rental costs, and other unexpected expenses, especially in the beginning. (The period it takes to build up a client base and awareness and trust from your neighborhood and community can be between one to three years, depending on the activity and profile of the school and the effectiveness of your marketing strategy.)

Your hours can be flexible according to your schedule or other responsibilities, such as a part-time job in the mornings. You could concentrate on teaching art classes in the afternoons, evenings, and weekends. On the other hand, if you rented a studio space, your hours might possibly be dictated by the owner of the building or the district in which your studio is located.

The best part of having a home-based studio is that you will not have to commute to work nor will you have the additional expenses of gas and car maintenance.

However, before you leap into transforming a space in your home into a studio, you should consider the disadvantages. First of all be aware that having a studio in your home gives it a "hobby" and "passion for the arts" feel, rather than seeming like a dynamic business that is constantly looking for more students. As well, some people find it harder to stop working for the day when their work is in their own home. It becomes tricky to set boundaries between personal life and business life. Your family may become upset when dinner or family time is interrupted by phone calls or when your attempt to accommodate your students' busy schedules for classes and other programs interferes. It may also cause problems when students show up unexpectedly to discuss a project or drop off a late assignment.

You must also consider the fact that your neighbors may not like having their parking spaces used, even for quick pickups and drop-offs of students. In fact, zoning restrictions may not allow you to have a home-based business (discussed in more detail later in this chapter).

You may also need to do some renovations to provide for adequate ventilation and lighting. This could be costly, but you may decide that the costs for redesigning a space are cheaper than renting.

When making any major decisions about my business I start by creating a "SCOT analysis" to understand all my strengths, challenges, opportunities, and threats. Sample 1 is an example of the SCOT analysis I created as I contemplated offering art classes from my first home studio.

## Renting studio space

You may feel that your home is not a suitable place for your business because of space constraints or family concerns. If this is the case, you will need to look for a suitable place outside of your home, in an area that will encourage clients to come to your business.

There are benefits to leasing a space for your studio and the location can be one of them. You may be able to acquire a space in an area that attracts lots of students from surrounding schools and colleges, or a busy retail area that attracts walk-by traffic. There may also be more parking spaces for your clients.

Another great advantage to renting is that when you leave your studio at the end of the day, your workday is done. No one will interrupt you at home in regard to business, because your business telephone number and address are different from that of your home. And this business address can go on all of your promotional material, such as your business cards and website. With a home-based studio, you wouldn't freely give out your personal contact information, as you would want to protect your family and neighbors from strangers making surprise visits to your home to see the studio.

The studio may already be set up with appropriate lighting and ventilation for your business, and you may have fewer costs when it comes to designing the space than you would in a home-based studio. However, you will have to consider whether or not your landlord will allow you to make any significant improvements to the studio; for example, painting the walls or adding appropriate flooring. You may also have restrictions in your lease regarding the size and placement of your advertising signs. (Always seek legal advice before signing a lease agreement.)

There are other disadvantages to renting. Safety can be an issue for you and your clients. Is the area safe at night? Are the parking area and bus stop well lit?

You will need to consider transportation as well. Since many of your students may be younger and unable drive, you will need to make sure there is a bus stop close by.

The biggest disadvantage of a rented studio is the costs, which include rent and

# SAMPLE 1
# SCOT ANALYSIS FOR JOLLY GOOD ART HOME-BASED STUDIO

| Strengths | Challenges |
|---|---|
| • In control of hours; able to work part-time or for as many hours as I choose<br>• Home for my daughter after school<br>• Neighborhood is a great location next to a reputable large school and a family-oriented population<br>• No pressure to pay rent and extra expenses associated with renting retail space | • Neighbors may not like added traffic outside my home — check zoning bylaws and parking regulations<br>• Lack of privacy: clients in home space even if it is in the basement; phone rings at all hours seven days a week<br>• No address on promotional leaflets and on website, giving only the phone number and geographical area of where classes are being offered<br>• Not being taken as seriously as the established competition with their business premises, campsites, and galleries in more prominent commercial locations<br>• Family sees me but cannot have the quality of attention they are used to |
| **Opportunities** | **Threats** |
| • Because of money saved by not paying rent and other retail site expenses, more profits can be injected toward improved programs, more art materials, and additional staff, which in turn will increases the number of programs offered<br>• Design or upgrade website to better market the business and bring brand awareness | • Zoning restrictions may not allow services or expansion<br>• Longevity; physical and Internet presence — I must keep up with trends and needs to stay on community's mind: regular art classes, seasonal programs, and unique parties<br>• Difficulty leaving work issues behind outside of working hours |

utilities. You may also have to lock into a year's lease or longer, which can be a problem when you are just starting out and you realize after a few months that you are not making enough money to pay for the space.

Complete Exercise 5, which will help you decide where you want to start your business.

## Zoning

Various rules apply in the different regions of the US and Canada when it comes to home-based businesses. Before going further and doing any in-depth research for the proposed business, check the zoning by-laws with your municipality. In some areas you may not be allowed to undertake a home-based business at all — especially in a congested city or neighborhood in which parking is a significant issue. Do not tempt trouble by overlooking this important point at the beginning. Stay on the safe side to eliminate unnecessary stress.

Because zoning laws differ from city to city, contact your local municipality for exact rules and restrictions for your type of business. If you are renting a studio, get the relevant information and find out about regulations before committing to or signing a contract. Telephone or go to your local municipal office or visit its website for specific zoning laws.

If, in the beginning, you have not taken proper measures and researched the potential area, and if a neighbor complains to the authorities, you may incur fines and be closed down. Do not take any chances; confirm everything at the outset. Also confirm matters regarding signage on or around your rented space. Make sure you have up-to-date details from your zoning and regulations office about the types of signs you are allowed to display for promotion.

Contact your local city hall or your county clerk for the specific requirements regarding your business, as well as your local Chamber of Commerce for any legal advice on permits or licenses.

## Consider your neighbors

If you respect your neighbors, then they should respect you, and you should feel confident in letting them know what your services are, and even what these services can do for their children and the community. I did not encounter any problems with my neighbors. I was lucky to have a large driveway in which small groups of students could be dropped off and picked up by their parents.

Make the outside of your home as appealing as you can: Trim the lawn and get rid of weeds in your garden beds. For a minimum amount of money and effort I planted annuals in pots, which brightened up the pathways and made the front and foyer of my home look inviting. First impressions count to your clients, and your neighbors will appreciate your effort as well.

With a rented studio you must consider what retail neighbors you have. You don't want to set up your business in an area with lots of bars or big warehouses. You want to be in an area in which your clients and your retail neighbors will respect your business.

## EXERCISE 5
# WHERE WILL YOU START YOUR BUSINESS?

Once you have made sure you are not breaking any laws, you should answer the following questions:

1. How feasible is it for you to have a home-based business?

2. How much space do you need to allocate for classes and other services?

3. What do you want your studio to say about you and your services?

4. Are you opening a small or large studio? Do a SCOT analysis (Strengths, Challenges, Opportunities, and Threats).

5. Will you rent or own an art studio? Do a SCOT analysis on the advantages and disadvantages of each.

6. Do a SCOT analysis of your readiness to offer classes.

# Your Business Name

I came up with the name "Jolly Good Art" when I was thinking about what set me apart from the rest of the local art establishments. People remembered me because of my British accent, so I wanted my name to be associated with England. The business name is a powerful marketing tool, and at this point I was already branding both myself and my art studio.

When I asked the students in one of my regular classes what they thought of the slogan "Love of Art Is a Very Good Start," Rashad, a studious nine-year-old artist, suggested I change it to "Love of Art Is a Jolly Good Start" — to echo the name of the school. I promptly did, greatly appreciating my student's input.

I hoped that the slogan went hand in hand with my mission statement. My school was to be a place of self-discovery and personal attention, dedicated to all aspects of art, including art appreciation and an understanding of what one can do with various media. I created a simple computer-generated logo of an easel to reflect the informal, fun, and educational nature of the services available.

Start offering your classes after registering your business's name, but do not rush into creating a logo before you have had a chance to try the name on for size. It may come to you immediately, or it may come to you in the middle of the night like it did to me. Exercise 6 will help you generate ideas relevant to naming your business.

The perfect name is an important branding and marketing tool. It is a potential client's first point of contact. When you have thought up a few names that you like, I suggest you conduct a business name search in the government databases as well as on the Internet.

## Conducting a business name search

Keep your name short and simple. The shorter the name, the easier it is for potential and current clients to remember. The following list includes some business names I like because they are fun and show what the business is about:

- Movement from Within — a yoga school
- Throwing a Fit — a pottery school
- Your Fired — pottery painting and firing (in a kiln) services
- Gordon of Eden — gardener and tree doctor
- Sew What? — sewing-related services
- Alice Beads — costume-jewelry-making services

Make sure to keep the future in mind if you plan to use your own name as part of the company name. This may make it difficult to sell the business as a franchise. Also some clients may expect you to always be there, rather than having your staff teach them.

When you have come up with your company name, if you are in the US you should make a trip to the local courthouse and file for a DBA (Doing Business As). It costs around $50 and is a simple application to complete.

# EXERCISE 6
# CHOOSING YOUR BUSINESS NAME

1. What do you want the name of your classes or art school to convey to prospective students, their parents, your suppliers, and people in the community?

2. What sets you apart that you can incorporate into your business name and image?

3. Write down as many business names as you can brainstorm and ask other people — including children — for ideas.

4. How much of your start-up budget can you allocate for a designer to create a professional logo for your business?

5. If paying for a company slogan and logo is not feasible, can you suggest a bartering arrangement with anyone who has these skills? What services can you offer in exchange?

The government website www.usa.gov will help you get started on all aspects of starting and registering your business in the US. The Small Business Administration (SBA) website (www.sba.gov) will also give you information and tips for registering your business.

In Canada, if you are incorporating your business, you will need to do a name search. In some provinces you can go online and do a search through the NUANS system (Newly Updated Automated Name Search), while in others you will need to complete a name reservation or approval request form through your local government registry. For more information you can go the government's Canada Business website at www.cbsc.org.

Make sure you research your state or province's requirements for business, including name registration, permits, and licenses. In the US, you will need to contact the IRS to acquire an employer identification number (EIN), which is similar to a social security number for businesses. In Canada, you will need to contact the Canada Revenue Agency (CRA) to acquire a business number (BN).

### Searching the Internet for your proposed business name

Search for your proposed business name on the Internet and find out if such a company already exists. I am a strong believer that Internet presence is essential to reaching a wider audience in your immediate community and beyond. Having a unique name can only help you in this regard.

Go to such sites as www.godaddy.com, www.networksolutions.com, or many others

on the market and buy the domain name you are interested in now even if you do not plan to create a website yet. It can be as cheap as $8 through some companies. (A large part of Chapter 7 is dedicated to why a website is important, and what work goes into the building and design of websites, particularly for an art school business.)

Do a search with various key words to see what other websites there are of companies that may have names that are similar to your own. You would not want to break any copyright, trademark, or other laws. Also, look at the results of possible search words your prospective clients or their children might use.

# Making Your Business Legal

Do some research and speak with professionals such as your accountant, your lawyer, or businesspeople in your social network to find out what you need to do to make your business legal. Get the appropriate licenses and liability insurance for your business before going any further.

### Incorporation and other business structures

Incorporating a business can help protect you personally from lawsuits and creditors. You will need to research this carefully, and you may want to hire a business lawyer to help you set up your business properly. You may also want to contact a certified accountant to help you with any tax issues that may arise from your company.

In the US, you can either create your business as an S corporation ("Inc.") or limited liability company ("LLC"). Creating an

S corporation or an LLC can shield you personally from lawsuits and creditors. For more information, go to www.sba.gov as well as www.ccr.gov (the Central Contractor Registration website).

In Canada, you can either incorporate your business or create a sole proprietorship. If you incorporate your business you will have limited liability, which means that you will be protected from creditors and lawsuits. If you choose to start out as a sole proprietorship, you will have lower start-up costs, but you must be aware that your company will have unlimited liability, that is, you will *not* be protected from creditors and lawsuits. You can always start as a sole proprietor and choose to incorporate your business as your company evolves.

In Canada you can also register as a partnership, which means you and your partner will share all the profits and losses of the business. If you decide to take on a partner, carefully consider all the advantages and disadvantages of doing so. Many small companies and businesses have people who run things internally but who may not have the capacity or desire to sell, market, promote, or be the front person, and vice versa. Make sure you and your partner have skills that complement each other's, and that the business is a good fit for both of your personalities.

## Sales tax registration

If you plan to sell art supplies, obtain accurate information regarding relevant taxes for buying and reselling goods, and make sure your zoning permit allows you to be selling products from your premises.

You will have to register for a sales tax number in advance. This applies in all states and provinces that have sales tax. Take the time to learn about record keeping of all incoming and outgoing documents, and how often you must file tax returns. With assistance from your accountant, you should be able to form an organized system, and maintain it with the least amount of disruption to your day.

To find out more information about sales taxes, go to your local government office or visit its website. There are also many good books at your local library or bookstore that cover the topics of collection and remittance of sales taxes. When in doubt, contact an accountant, who will be aware of the latest tax regulations.

## Liability insurance

Have an in-depth discussion with a home or business insurance agent in your area. Shop around for the best plans and figure out exactly what type of coverage your business needs. Give the insurance agent all the details, making it clear exactly what you plan to do in the business and at the premises. You will find that there are precise safety regulations. Also ask a seasoned business associate for advice based on what he or she had to go through.

I made sure that I obtained the highest-liability insurance coverage available, and I advise you to do the same. The premiums are not costly, and it is essential that your school be completely insured against liability, in case of any student or staff injuries. This is particularly true if you are not a limited liability company.

## Police check

A large number of your students will probably be children. To help alleviate some of the valid concerns parents and school boards may have, you should undergo a criminal record check. For more information, contact your local police department. There is a cost for the service, which varies depending on your location.

You should also request your prospective employees to do the same. I recommend that you always verify their references as well. These people are coming in under the umbrella of your school. Do your homework at the beginning. Keep the children in your care as safe as you possibly can.

# 2

# BECOMING A MULTIFACETED ENTREPRENEUR

*What one does, one becomes.*

— SPANISH PROVERB

As you get started with your business, you also have to take a long, hard look at yourself. Do you have what it takes to be an entrepreneur?

I define *entrepreneur* as an industrious, resourceful, tenacious individual who leaves no stone unturned when it comes to achieving his or her highest goals. All an entrepreneur cares about is when, where, and how to succeed. For the entrepreneur, competition is a way of life and perseverance is second nature. Failure is not an option. And an entrepreneur gets to the top with integrity and by being aware of how one's actions affect the community at large.

Although there is no guarantee, the more you put into your business, the more you achieve. It is your choice if you spend your days working in a nine-to-five job, and going home to relax in front of the TV. If you want to achieve something more in your life, however, then take the steps to make your dreams become reality. Remember that a journey of a thousand miles starts with one step.

## Characteristics of an Entrepreneur

Being an entrepreneur means adapting to the trends and demands of the business environment. You must apply the skills you excel at and learn to constantly exceed your own expectations, and you must also learn how to do new and specialized things (which other professionals can do for you eventually as your business grows). If you are lacking in some skills, act quickly to acquire them. Or at least find ways around this to accelerate the start-up and actual running of the business.

Doing everything yourself in the beginning is a good way for you to understand the daily running of all aspects of your business. When you are ready to delegate some of these activities, you will have control over and insight into them. The following list contains six different roles of an entrepreneur that you will take on when your start your business:

- Student/Learner
- Architect/Designer
- Administrator/Implementer
- Politician/Negotiator
- Coach/Mentor
- Wizard/Miracle Worker

Let's break down what each of these entrepreneurial roles represents:

As a *student* you will need to —

- listen to your customers (i.e., your students and their parents) and pay attention to your staff's needs and suggestions about how to continually improve the business,
- deal with different personalities and behaviors,
- improve your decision-making strategies,
- conduct market research to improve services, and

- conduct self-evaluations and continue personal development.

As an *architect* you will need to —

- be a visionary,
- be strategic, precise, and a creative business planner,
- set short- and long-term goals,
- create and implement innovative programs, and
- be a web designer.

As an *administrator* you will need to —

- organize your business processes (e.g., accounting and bookkeeping),
- organize and stock inventory (such as art supplies), and
- manage time and make things happen.

As a *politician* you will need to —

- be a hybrid of a diplomat and salesperson,
- make good first impressions,
- keep clients returning,
- attract new clients,
- understand and deliver what clients really need,
- network and communicate with clients, potential clients, staff, and other professionals that you will come in contact with,
- be an effective negotiator who can close a deal,
- strive to keep everyone happy, and
- resolve conflicts.

As a *coach* you will need to —

- be a cheerleader and mentor by bringing out the best in all your contacts (i.e., clients, parents, staff, suppliers, and partners),

- be an active listener,

- be a human resources expert, training and motivating staff,

- uphold strict moral codes as well as personal and professional integrity, and

- express your visions for the business to staff and partners.

As a *wizard* you will need to —

- be a miracle worker and multitasker who juggles all of the above roles (i.e., student, architect, administrator, politician, and coach), and

- be a resourceful and creative problem solver with a winning attitude.

These entrepreneurial roles are interconnected and, therefore, overlaps may occur. The wizard coordinates and juggles the many traits of the entrepreneur. If one hat best fits your personality or mood most of the time, and you neglect the other aspects of your business, the resulting imbalance can pose a risk of failure. The following example will help you understand the importance of being able to use a combination of the characteristics mentioned above.

---

Let's say you plan a big craft fair to raise money for charity. Planning this event requires all of your *architect* skills. A craft fair provides an opportunity for your students to showcase their art projects and for their parents to feel pride in their accomplishments. Your students may bring their siblings, friends, and other prospective students to your school, and linking the craft fair to a charity involves the community as a whole. Journalists are always hungry to cover stories that showcase the community's successes, and if money is raised for a charity, the event will be greatly appreciated.

For this charity event you also use your *politician* skills to attract people to your event. You have your creative juices flowing. But then what happens? You fail to organize the art supplies, which means that you have failed as an *administrator*. You have let everyone down, and have also hurt your school's reputation. You will have your work cut out for you to reestablish your credibility. This could be very costly, because prospective clients judge your school on first impressions. A perfect opportunity to boost business awareness has just been wasted. The adage bears repeating: "If you fail to prepare, prepare to fail."

---

Complete Exercise 7 to find out if you are ready to become an entrepreneur.

It is important for each of us to know our own limitations and strengths and how to use them most effectively. We tend to concentrate on doing things that we are good at and enjoy, neglecting or avoiding the things that we do not particularly like to do until we are eventually forced to address the massive backlog.

# EXERCISE 7
# ARE YOU AN ENTREPRENEUR?

Circle the letters beside the answers that most accurately reflect your experience.

1. What type of worker are you?
   a) I prefer to work for a company as an employee.
   b) I think outside the box and like stirring up controversy.
   c) I thrive on seeking out opportunities to improve the way I work and enhance the success of my endeavors.

2. What best describes your working habits in your past or present business enterprise?
   a) I always pace myself so that my job does not rule me.
   b) I become overwhelmed and even risk my health in order to succeed.
   c) I feel held back from accomplishing more.

3. What did you learn about money in your early adolescence?
   a) That life is more secure when I have a regular income.
   b) That life is much more intriguing if I take more risks and follow the exciting path of unpredictable highs and lows.
   c) That money is recognized as an indicator of success.

4. What best describes your experience when you were a student?
   a) I excelled in most of my subjects and mainly followed the rules.
   b) I did not see any point in taking exams.
   c) I made it through exams with difficulty.

5. What do you think about formal education?
   a) Formal education is very important to get ahead.
   b) Doing something and learning through experience are much more important than formal training.
   c) A blend of formal education and experience will bring the success and motivation I seek.

6. If you had the opportunity to start your own company, what would you do?
   a) I would calculate and recalculate the risks and then put my idea aside. Life gets in the way and owning a business is too risky.
   b) I would analyze all the risks, enlist the opinions of trusted successful entrepreneurs, and then initiate a business plan and start the ball rolling.
   c) I would see an open opportunity to make a fresh start and change my life.

7. How do you work with your colleagues and network of contacts?
   a) I am a good team member, but I'm usually not a leader and sometimes I feel frustrated because I want to take hold of the reins.
   b) I love to get involved, to help, and to make a difference.
   c) My colleagues and I work well together because we have mutual trust and respect for one another.

8. Are you a good mentor or coach?
   a) I prefer to work as a member of a team so that I can rely on my colleagues to share the responsibilities.
   b) As a manager I'm very task focused and want to achieve my objectives as quickly as possible and to the best of my abilities.
   c) I love to inspire those around me by setting realistic goals for them and seeing them excel in all their endeavors.

9. What does volunteering mean to you?
   a) Helping out at the occasional school activities or at my child's sporting events.
   b) Helping the community to make an impact on a small or large scale, whenever and wherever possible — but sometimes I get distracted and off track.
   c) It's a healthy obligation to help those less fortunate.

10. What do you do when something goes wrong in your personal life or at work?
   a) I get frustrated and cannot think of any solutions.
   b) I avoid conflict whenever possible and hope it does not rear its ugly head.
   c) I see it as yet another challenge presented by the unpredictability of life and roll back my sleeves to resolve issues.

## Taking Stock of Your Answers

### You selected mainly A

If you answered mainly A, you are either a very adaptable soul who will do well on many levels in a small or large business or a low risk taker who has learned from life that security is of prime importance. If you are ingrained in this way of thinking, be careful about venturing out alone into the exciting but unpredictable world of self-employment or business ownership. Why not consider partnering up with someone whose spark and creativity will keep you running on the hot coals of the demands and changeability of running a business. Learn to balance the dichotomy of being levelheaded and creative.

If you are interested in leaving your current position that is relatively secure, if you have been made redundant, or if you believe the grass on the entrepreneurial turf is greener and more profitable, then tread softly and do as much preliminary homework as you can. If all your analysis and gut instincts tell you to go for it, then make sure you have a grounded knowledge of the different aspects of owning a business.

The advantage of being coolheaded is that you will not let impulse and your exciting new ideas get you into major problems by overextending yourself.

**You selected mainly B**

If you answered mainly B, you have either been an entrepreneur or you have dreamed about it for so long that you are ready to jump in with both feet. You have definitely got the personality, drive, tenacity, and lack of fear of rejection, but you also sometimes suffer from trying to do too much too soon.

The advantage of being this committed and determined is that your creativity, vision, and enthusiasm will take you through to success much sooner than a person who may be hesitant or overly cautious. You are positive most of the time. You love interacting with people and always achieve what you want when you set your mind to it.

Watch out for the entrepreneur's "get up and go" attitude — this may need to be contained sometimes. Sometimes you may be tempted to do too much, too soon. To be true to your vision you will need to learn to rein yourself in. Get more organized, and stop to take time to enjoy your current success. In other words, pace yourself. This is where a grounded partner, trusted mentor, or a coach can be of immense help. Your creative spirit knows how to soar and make things happen, and all you need to do is learn how to prioritize, set aside your impulsive "anything's possible" attitude, and go ahead with a new goal or expansion idea after much levelheaded consideration of facts and your actions' consequences.

Rest assured, you are an entrepreneur with tremendous ability and talent to inspire those around you so that they will want to work with you and learn from you.

**You selected mainly C**

If you answered mainly C, you have an advantage over the other two types of personalities. You have a grounded, realistic attitude, and once you put your mind to something, you calculate the risks, take steps to make things happen, and keep a cautious eye on your progress.

There may have been times when opportunities have come along but you were not in a position to take advantage of them. Fear of failure may have interrupted your entrepreneurial momentum. You have not always been certain of your abilities to see something through. Now, with your life experiences and transferable skills as well as your maturity, you are at a different, positive place. Your expertise and network group guarantee ongoing support, as you are known as a trustworthy and fair person.

You have admirable people skills and determination to make a difference, so you can master those other challenges. If you are determined to get help, to learn to delegate more effectively, and to hone your confidence and faith in your abilities, success will come to you that much sooner.

Concentrate on your major life goals with the help of a professional such as a coach or mentor. Then research facts and opportunities and move toward realizing your goals. No one but you can be in control of your destiny.

Take a good long look at your skills and realize that in order for your school to earn a great reputation, you and your staff have to impart the right messages, whether they are literal or subconscious. The right attitude is imperative. Become aware of and address those weaknesses that may stand in the way of your success.

What differentiates great companies from good ones? The attitudes and commitment of their staff. If you are not a natural team leader or you find it hard to motivate and manage people, bone up on these skills before starting your business, instead of just jumping in and hoping for the best. With a strong will, incentive, and confidence at the outset, you can achieve success sooner rather than later.

## Your Strengths and Challenges at the Beginning

Everyone has fears of some form, and some of these fears may grow to become phobias. My fears are left over from having been brought up in a hardworking but financially insecure family, and have resulted in my vowing never to depend on anyone as much as I depend on myself. For a number of years I had worked as an administrative assistant and office manager, and this experience confirmed for me that there are those who should be employees and those who should be their own bosses. I am one of the latter.

Some people are content to work in the background, satisfied with receiving recognition in the form of pay and respect, and do not feel compelled to be in charge of anything but the office equipment. Their pride in a job well done with no hassle outside of their nine-to-five hours is sufficient for them.

Others, however, become restless, resentful, and unhappy with their situation. Unable to stop at the notion that "this is just a job," they instead feel compelled to do everything to the best of their abilities and strive for more recognition. Their current positions may not give them sufficient challenges or satisfaction. These people are goal-oriented and aspire to move up the corporate ladder, or to start their own businesses in the future. But no matter how many promotions they get, they still search for new hurdles to overcome. These are people who need to be their own bosses.

Make a list of your biggest and most redeeming assets, strengths, and traits. Include such characteristics as using calm logic while everyone around you is becoming stressed. Consider your organizational skills, people skills, and creativity.

To prepare yourself for the next section on personal skills development, complete Exercise 8. This exercise will help you focus on what areas you feel confident about and what areas you may need to work on. And then take a look at Sample 2, a SCOT analysis I did of my own personality when I started my business.

## Personal Skills Development

As an entrepreneur, you may need to develop new skills or improve upon existing ones. Most of us need to face numerous challenges, on a regular basis. Some of these challenges may include conquering our fears of public speaking, overcoming shyness, and learning to delegate tasks.

# EXERCISE 8
## PERSONALITY STRENGTHS AND CHALLENGES

Place a check mark in all the columns that apply to you. In order for this exercise to be of true benefit, answer honestly rather than selecting what you hope will be the best answer.

| Characteristics | Always | Sometimes | Rarely | Never |
|---|---|---|---|---|
| I am a loner. | | | | |
| I am introverted. | | | | |
| I am motivated. | | | | |
| I am a good multitasker. | | | | |
| I am decisive. | | | | |
| I am committed. | | | | |
| I am self-confident. | | | | |
| I am hardworking. | | | | |
| I am creative. | | | | |
| I am a creative troubleshooter. | | | | |
| I am a strong communicator. | | | | |
| I am a strong negotiator. | | | | |
| I am a good listener. | | | | |
| I am a good boss. | | | | |
| I am independent. | | | | |
| I am a good salesperson. | | | | |
| I am resourceful. | | | | |
| I am a flexible teacher and supervisor. | | | | |
| I am organized. | | | | |
| I am tenacious. | | | | |
| I am emotional. | | | | |
| I am a good team builder. | | | | |
| I am a risk taker. | | | | |
| I am health-conscious. | | | | |
| I am logical. | | | | |
| I motivate others. | | | | |
| I encourage others. | | | | |
| I like meeting new people. | | | | |
| I procrastinate. | | | | |
| I handle stress well. | | | | |
| I see an idea through to the finish. | | | | |
| I plan ahead. | | | | |
| I delegate appropriately. | | | | |
| I overdelegate. | | | | |
| I underdelegate. | | | | |
| I like to be in charge. | | | | |
| I help others to thrive. | | | | |
| I help others find their own capabilities and talents. | | | | |

**Taking Stock of Your Answers**

Be proud of your obvious talents and what you do well. What can you see as major points that could cause problems in the near future? Are there any themes? If you are a procrastinator, or if you do not plan ahead effectively, or if you are not as organized as you would like to be, what is the best way for you to work to accomplish tasks?

Would you consider being accountable to a coach or a trusted friend who will check up on your promised progress? Try this for a short time; perhaps weekly for two months.

Another method would be to use a simple time-management calendar on your computer that flashes a reminder of what you need to do every time you turn on the computer. Of course this will only be effective if you make a strong commitment to input and update the actions regularly and to use these reminders until following through becomes second nature. For more detailed suggestions on time management, read Chapter 10, Get Organized and Stay Organized.

If you are not as health-conscious as you would like to be, your business could suffer in the long run, especially if the drive to succeed takes priority over everything else. Learning to balance and schedule time out of a day or a week for recharging could make a huge difference in your business and in your personal life.

If you do not delegate enough tasks and do not have the interpersonal skills to effectively motivate others, you must commit to learning these skills. By doing so, you will accomplish more than if you simply continue on and hope for the best.

Take note of all your strengths and put them to good use.

If your determination to succeed is powerful enough, you will be able to overcome any inner and external obstacles. Concentrate on points that need attention and find ways to improve on them so that you can build an unshakable foundation for your business.

## SAMPLE 2
# AUTHOR'S PERSONALITY SCOT ANALYSIS

| Strengths | Challenges |
|---|---|
| • Creative<br>• Not afraid to try new things<br>• Belief in myself and faith in process<br>• Do not take rejection personally<br>• Intuitive<br>• Optimistic | • Sometimes get bogged down and distracted by details of the business<br>• Do not file documents often enough<br>• Do not always appreciate my successes<br>• Second-guess myself when overwhelmed or stressed<br>• Have difficulty leaving work issues behind outside of working hours |
| **Opportunities** | **Threats** |
| • Gregarious personality brings me in more contact with various prospects and networking opportunities<br>• Not shy to try new collaborative methods and ideas with willing partners and staff | • Sabotage myself with too many details and forget my goals<br>• Sometimes the challenges become too much and personal relationships (family) suffer<br>• Physical health can suffer<br>• Disorganization can cause major problems |

## Public speaking

Some people enjoy standing up and speaking in front of a crowd. For others, there couldn't be anything more frightening. Fear of public speaking is one of the top five causes of anxiety, topping fear of death, financial ruin, and creepy crawly things!

You may not fear public speaking, but you may be slightly uncomfortable with other aspects of interacting with large groups. You may be shy by nature, or you may be afraid of rejection or of trying the unknown. Some of us are merely afraid of what we have not practiced before. Regardless, as an entrepreneur you will have to develop your public speaking skills in the search for long-lasting success. And you never know, you may discover that you actually enjoy public speaking and add it to your growing list of talents.

The benefits of learning and developing this skill far outweigh the investment of the extra time you spend on it. For me, these benefits included:

• Gaining the confidence to approach and speak to people from all walks of life and different business backgrounds

• Learning to listen effectively

• Learning to focus on my clients' reactions and needs

- Learning to speak about any subject at the spur of the moment

- Improving my interpersonal skills (for both my personal and business life)

I had decided to work on my public speaking skills when the date of the second annual Jolly Good Art exhibition approached. Although I was comfortable meeting with new students and their parents, I was still nervous about speaking in front of a large group of people in my studio.

When I first heard of Toastmasters, a nonprofit organization that helps people improve their public speaking and leadership skills, it meant nothing to me. Now, however, I was running a successful, expanding business. As the school's owner and leader, I had to stand up and speak eloquently and confidently about my business, which meant moving out of my personal comfort zone.

Toastmasters has a strong reputation for helping people from all walks of life gain insight into their communication styles and confidence in self-expression and the art of persuasion. This new path to self-discovery opened up more opportunities for me than I had ever expected. Not only did practicing public speaking help my confidence level, joining Toastmasters also increased my network of acquaintances — I found a diverse mix of minds and interests.

### Tips and techniques to become a better public speaker

Visualize, prepare, practice, and perfect: these are the four cornerstones that are essential to effective public speaking.

### Visualize

Visualize yourself speaking to hundreds of clients — whether it is at the yearly art exhibition, charity gala, or award evening. Keep in mind that public speaking is an aid to your business and personal development. You must also believe in yourself and your own expertise.

### Prepare

Study Toastmasters manuals and read as many books on the subject of public speaking as you can. (See the appendix for suggested reading.) You should also look up books on body language, humor, entertainment, education, and assertiveness/self-improvement. (Attending courses in the latter is also a good idea.) These topics will help you in the many avenues of business: You will learn to interact more effectively with those around you as well as gain more confidence figuring out what your clients want and need. Forgo TV or your recreational time for self-development — you are investing in your future!

### Practice

Prepare your speeches thoroughly and practice them in front of your family members and even a mirror. Give it your best. Practicing helps even acutely shy people overcome their stuttering and blushing.

Try to follow these tips in order to be completely prepared:

- Be interactive; take the initiative to address the audience.

- Act confident by smiling, and vary the tone of your voice. Perform like you are enjoying yourself and the crowd will love it.

- Learn to "read" your audience. This will give you a tremendous boost and will become easier as you gain experience.

### Perfect

The following tips will help you perfect your public speaking skills:

- Believe in yourself. You have information others will learn from and they will respect your opinion.

- Learn to push yourself out of your comfort zone.

- Do not second-guess yourself; follow your instincts and do what feels right. You know yourself best.

## Shyness and fear of rejection

Who do you really admire in your community or in your circle of friends and family? Who do you emulate in terms of profession, spiritual beliefs, or ethics?

Even if you think this person may not be able to spare his or her valuable time, what is the worst that can happen if you ask for his or her advice? He or she may direct you to someone who could help you. As far as I am concerned, getting a "No, sorry," reply is better than to hear years later: "You never asked; I'd have been more than happy to help."

Do not let shyness steal opportunities away from you or prematurely strip you of your chance for success just because you are afraid to be rejected. If you ask diplomatically for help and support, you may find that people are flattered that you hold them in such high regard. (There are more in-depth guidelines about mentorship and mentoring others in Chapter 9, Networking.)

Complete Exercise 9 to find out your level of comfort when it comes to connecting with other people. Take stock of your answers and know that your passion and love of what you do — art, teaching, and imparting your knowledge — are what will drive you out of your comfort zone. With experience your inner strength and confidence will grow. Have faith in your core beliefs and surround yourself with those who can help you grow even more resilient.

## Learning to delegate

If you want your company to grow, and you want to gain long-term benefits, you have to learn to delegate. This comes with a good support system and committed staff, and your trust in them. Learn to let go of all the different tasks that you have been doing alone. If you have family and reliable staff, enlist their help and cooperation. If you are already benefiting from the help of assistants, occasional or seasonal staff, or teachers with specific qualifications (e.g., in special needs education), then you have already seen the rewards. (Read Chapter 8 for advice on hiring employees.)

When you have established your business, you will probably want to hire an accountant or a bookkeeper. He or she can help you keep your finances in order while you spend your time doing other things to increase your business.

You may also consider hiring a lawyer for legal advice on such matters as zoning laws, and for dealing with liability issues. He or she will be up to date on current laws and will save you time researching and understanding complicated insurance forms and legal issues that may arise.

# EXERCISE 9
# SHYNESS AND ASSERTIVENESS

1.  When you are in a social gathering and someone in your small group offers a personal opinion that you strongly disagree with, what do you do?
    a)  I stay silent because I feel that I won't be listened to anyway.
    b)  I make a diplomatic observation that will not offend anyone, but I still make my point.
    c)  I go home stewing and frustrated at my own inability to assert myself, thinking of all the responses I could have made but did not.

2.  In a group of more than four people, either in a social- or business-related gathering, perhaps you stutter, blush, and cannot seem to string sentences together. If so, what do you do?
    a)  I ask myself, What is the worst that could happen in this situation?
    b)  I accept that I am never going to be able to speak in public.
    c)  I take steps to become a more effective communicator.

3.  Referring back to question 2, what positive options are open to you?
    *   Can you take a course in assertiveness training to gain confidence?
    *   Can you take a course in your field to increase your knowledge?
    *   Are there books or audiotapes that you can buy or borrow?
    *   Can you join a public-speaking club?
    *   Can you join a support group to overcome shyness?
    *   Ideally, what kind of group would you find most helpful for your personal and entrepreneurial enhancement?

4.  What types of hobbies would you like to try if you were less shy? If you didn't have any time or money constraints right now, what would you really like to pursue? (This does not have to be connected with your current ventures. For example, it can be as far removed as kayaking, knitting, yoga, or origami.)

5.  What is holding you back from pursuing one of the hobbies identified in question 4? List at least 15 reasons that come to mind. You may want to check off some of the items in the following list and add additional things holding you back.
    [  ]  Given the time I spend on my business, spending even more time away from my family is neither feasible nor fair.
    [  ]  I am too tired or not in the right frame of mind.
    [  ]  I cannot think of anything that is worth pursuing.
    [  ]  Hobbies will distract me from my goals, both business and personal.
    [  ]  I am too shy.

[   ]   I am too different.

[   ]   I am boring.

[   ]   I am afraid to try anything drastically different.

[   ]   My hobby idea has nothing to do with my business and none of my family do it or like the idea.

[   ]   Other: _____
_____

[   ]   Other: _____
_____

[   ]   Other: _____
_____

6.   Is there a mentor or coach that you respect and trust who can start you on a new regime of replacing bad habits with energizing and positive ones?

**Taking Stock of Your Answers**

Every businessperson, no matter how experienced, has strengths and areas that need to be developed. Review your answers to the questions above. Do you see a theme in your strengths and in areas you could improve on? For example, do you shy away from certain social interactions for fear of conflict?

Other exercises in this book, may help you to conquer some, if not most, of the skills for optimum success that you lack. The fact that you are constantly striving to improve will lead to greater accomplishments.

As will be discussed in Chapter 7, Creating Your Web Presence, you may also want to delegate your website design (and all of the updating this entails) to a professional web designer. This could save you many hours of research and frustration!

For personal support (in addition to any family cooperation you may have), I suggest you consider hiring domestic help. At first, doing so may seem unnecessary or too expensive, but I found that a cleaner every two weeks kept the house in order and my housekeeping duties to a minimum. Each visit meant that I saved four or five hours of cleaning time. I could then spend more time on other business-related activities such as networking and mining for more prospective clients. Or I could spend that time recharging or being with my family.

## Learning Styles

We are each unique and have individual learning styles based on our personalities, our life experiences, and our environment. There are three methods of interpreting everything and everyone around us:

- Visual
- Auditory
- Physical

Usually one method is predominant for a person, and this becomes his or her learning style; also, we sometimes adopt a different learning style according to circumstances. (Exercise 10 will help you to understand your own learning style as well as that of your students.) Another common way to categorize learning styles is by "left brain" (responsible for logic and fact processing) and "right brain" (responsible for creativity, imagination, and intuition). There is no right or wrong method to learning — it just depends on what works best for you. Although our preferred habits of learning and interacting with others are ingrained, we can develop other skills or hone existing ones.

So you may be a true artist at heart with the classic tendency to use the right (creative) side of your brain, or you may lean more toward using the left side (all about logic, facts, and details). And what about your students? You must learn how to match your teaching style to your students, and how best to stimulate them. This insight into your behavior and the behavior of those around you is invaluable for your life as a businessperson, teacher, and artist.

Studies show that when it comes to decision making, the right-brain-dominant people are guided and influenced by their emotions and their intuition while left-brain-dominant people depend on their logic and sequential thinking. Obviously this affects how we study and learn as well as how we conduct our business and personal lives. Knowing how your entrepreneurial brain works helps you make informed and confident decisions. Good decisions are made when you are aware of all your strengths and weaknesses, and of where your ideas come from (whether they are artistic ideas or business ideas).

Understanding your students' learning styles will help you adjust your own teaching methods to get the best results from the students. But remember that each person is unique and has a mix of learning styles, and can adapt and use other techniques too. For more detailed information on the many different learning styles, visit www.learning -styles-online.com.

# EXERCISE 10
# LEARNING STYLES

Circle the letter beside the answer that most accurately reflects your learning style.

1.  What do you consider to be your best method of studying?
    a)  Underlining, circling, or highlighting important points.
    b)  Writing or recording information and listening to and repeating facts to myself.
    c)  Re-enacting or discussing facts about artwork seen, copied, or photographed.
    d)  A combination of some or all of the above.

2.  What do you like to use to learn new art techniques?
    a)  Photographs, artwork, and/or videos about the masters to inspire me.
    b)  Audiotapes of teachers' explanations of facts and theories, and repeating the information to myself.
    c)  Discussions and role-play, and then painting, practicing, and experimenting.
    d)  A combination of some or all of the above.

3.  Which is the best way for you to remember something?
    a)  Watching demonstrations in class or on video.
    b)  Listening and discussing what I've seen and heard about other peoples' practices.
    c)  Experimenting and practicing the lesson. I would rather touch the exhibits I am studying than sit still in a classroom.
    d)  A combination of some or all of the above.

4.  Which way do you work best?
    a)  I like to be surrounded by inspiring paintings and art materials that help me conjure up images to help me with my ideas or projects.
    b)  When I am conceptualizing and collecting my thoughts, I like to talk to others about my ideas and listen to music that inspires my creativity. When I'm in detail mode, I prefer to work in silence or with unobtrusive music.
    c)  I like to work in chaos and listen to loud music while experimenting and sharing with people around me.
    d)  A combination of some or all of the above.

5.  How do you prepare when you have to go somewhere you've never been to before?
    a)  I use a map.
    b)  I use an electronic navigation system or ask someone for directions.
    c)  I find the place the day before so that I am confident that I will find it when I have an appointment.
    d)  A combination of some or all of the above.

## EXERCISE 10 — CONTINUED

### Taking Stock of Your Answers

**You selected mainly A**

If you answered mainly A, you are predominantly a visual learner. As a visual learner, you are good at recognizing faces and have a good sense of direction. You are fashion-conscious and are very astute at picking up other people's body language.

When creating art, you need time to form your ideas in your mind's eye and tap into your imagination. You have an affinity for colors and mixing them to your preferred shades. You like to take lots of notes and highlight or underline sections that are especially important to you in art literature.

You are a good speller and like to use charts and spreadsheets when studying.

You love to read and watch videos. You enjoy learning from instructional art videos and teachers' demonstration during class. Index cards are very useful to you.

You often say, "I see what you mean" or "I get the picture."

**You selected mainly B**

If you answered mainly B, you are predominantly an auditory learner. As an auditory learner you like to read out loud and talk to yourself, as well as speaking out and participating in class. You are very expressive and are a good listener most of the time. You are attuned to small nuances in people's voices and to the tones of paintings, books, and movies.

You remember people's names and you prefer to hear someone give you directions to a new place rather than using a map. You prefer to listen to lectures rather than to write down notes. You prefer oral tests to written ones.

Music is very important to you, and most of the time you have the stereo turned on. You study or paint to background music or with the TV turned on. Certain types of music affect your mood. You learn a lot by listening to recorded lectures and watching videos as well as by repeating information back to yourself with your eyes closed.

You often say, "I hear what you're saying" or "that sounds like a plan."

**You selected mainly C**

If you answered mainly C, you are predominantly a physical learner. You learn the most by experiencing and acting out things. You are energetic and sporty, but you are not the best of spellers. You also sometimes miss points when reading or writing. Your handwriting is not the neatest.

You love scientific experimentation as well as jumping into a new art project and seeing what develops. Sculpture, vibrant shapes, and colors really fill your sense of the dramatic.

You express yourself through your body language and use your hands a lot when speaking. You can get impatient or fidgety when on a long journey or in long lectures.

You prefer to participate in stimulating class discussions as well as in group activities such as dance, karate, yoga, or drama. If given a choice, you would visit art galleries and study artists' works that inspire you instead of going to class. You also prefer to touch exhibits and explore the world, rather than sitting in class studying about theory.

You like to say, "I think that's a great idea" or "I feel that ..."

**You selected combinations of A, B, and C**
If you have a combination of physical and auditory styles, you may rely on both these styles more than you rely on your visual skills. For example, you may like to use music as stimulation to practice or paint a piece you are studying, and use role-playing. The visual student may like to rely more on the images in his or her head, visualizing the end results before starting on a project.

Many people learn the most through experience and by "doing." The combination of doing, speaking about what we have learned, making notes, and referring to them is the ideal way of ensuring a higher retention of information.

A person with a combination of all three learning styles would be an analytical, imaginative, hands-on, and dynamic learner.

# Other Things to Consider

Having a dream or passion to start a business and envisioning yourself thriving in it does not always guarantee success. Faced with unpredictable highs and lows and obstacles big and small, we have to be tenacious on our journey.

Your insights into your strengths and challenges may make you stand out in the crowd. But do you have staying power? That depends on whether or not you have a passion for your calling and a voracious hunger to succeed.

People start their own art businesses for a variety of reasons, which include the following:

- They love art and enjoy imparting their knowledge.
- They want to teach part time to supplement their current income.
- They want to work from home and be close to their children.

Some people are determined to sink every cent they earn back into their business for as long as it takes them to establish a large and healthy clientele. Some people persevere even when there is not much money coming in, and it is obviously stated in the accounts reports at the end of the quarter or year. Others concentrate their efforts on attracting as many new prospects as possible to ensure a strong foundation and a thriving business. And some start small by feeling their way toward growth and expansion. Others buy an existing start-up business.

You have to decide what you are prepared to do and what your level of commitment is. If you find yourself making too many excuses, and flopping down in front of the hypno-tube (aka the TV) to relax, wishing, in the back of your mind, that you had the guts or stamina for this project that really inspired you at one point, then you are ready for a reality check. You need to get off that sofa and get into a new routine, both for your business and your health! My first advice is to start exercising — try taking a 20-minute walk first thing in the morning — and you will soon have the energy to undertake the next exciting step in your business.

If you have a young and/or demanding family, support and time to devote to your business can be tricky to find. When your kids are involved in extracurricular activities, do you have time to yourself? Or do you have to stay and supervise your child the whole time he or she practices dance, yoga, or karate? Or if you are single, do you have parents or friends who pressure you to spend your weekends and evenings with them?

Maybe you can look for a support system from other members of the family. Or think about close friends, a social group you meet through your hobbies, or a support group (e.g., a parents network). If you are a single parent or a working mother trying to start your own business but have no spare time, look into bartering. A friend or relative with children can look after your kids in return for an agreed number of art classes. You get to spend a few uninterrupted hours developing or instigating your business ideas, and your friend is paid with art lessons he or she has always wanted, but could not otherwise afford. It is a win-win situation.

You must also have "me" time, personal time that has nothing to do with the business; otherwise your resource well will start to run dry. In extreme cases you may end up sacrificing your health and experience stress overload. (See the section Risks and Signs of Burnout in Chapter 10.)

Complete Exercise 11 and find out if you have what it takes to be an entrepreneur.

With some help from others, I believe we are able to discover exactly what each of us needs in order to excel. There is no clear boundary that separates the business part of the brain from the creative part, although you may indeed be more of a left- or right-brained thinker (i.e., creative and artistic versus logical). Try the opposite to how you naturally respond to situations — using "all of your brain" is the most effective way to meet challenges. If we put our thoughts into action, we will quickly get feedback to confirm that we are on the right track. This in turn brings confidence. With time, you will learn to trust that positive gut feeling, and to just go for it.

Of course, I am not suggesting that you spontaneously kick the boss in the teeth and quit your job on the grounds that you are a born entrepreneur, and shock your spouse or family into catatonic stupor with your wish to "live your dream." Discuss and expand on your ideas with those whose lives may be impacted by your plans. Communication is of the utmost importance at every stage of the process, especially at the conception and start-up phase of your art teaching business. Whatever your situation — whether you are a new entrepreneur, a single parent, or a seasoned businessperson — you need to set up an effective support system around you. The two goals of making a living and building your business have to be considered together. To secure the support of a spouse, mentor, or partner, in-depth communication and discussion need to take place.

The following example outlines a situation that can happen if you and your spouse are not open and honest with each other.

---

Elizabeth, a married mother of two teenagers, explained that although her husband had not stopped her in her endeavors to start her e-art business (having considered it her little project), he did not like the increasing amounts of time it was taking away from her household duties. He started subtly sabotaging her hours and made discouraging remarks that she found upsetting and unsettling.

"The more successful I became the more he resented my business," Elizabeth explained. "When I tried to discuss what the real issue was he'd deny there was anything wrong — until I got my break to transfer my home business to a retail space."

The marriage suffered to such an extent that it eventually ended in divorce. It took Elizabeth a few years before she realized that her business had not caused the rift, and that she had taken all the steps possible to remedy any marital problems as they surfaced. The underlying issues were that her husband had not liked her change from a dutiful wife and mother to a self-assured and independent businesswoman.

---

# EXERCISE 11
# DO YOU HAVE WHAT IT TAKES?

1.  Are you good at expressing yourself in the following situations? (Answer yes or no.)
    a)  Business concerns _____
    b)  Personal situations and issues _____

2.  How much do you enjoy imparting knowledge and experience to others? (Check the appropriate box.)
    [   ]   Always
    [   ]   Sometimes
    [ . ]   Rarely

3.  Apart from work- and family-related activities, what are your three favorite activities? What satisfaction do you get from these activities?


4.  Which age group do you most enjoy teaching? (Check the appropriate box.) Explain why. (You need to understand your own capabilities and how you can work with them.)
    [   ]   Children
    [   ]   Adolescents
    [   ]   Adults

5.  Would your teaching style suit younger or older children? (Keep in mind that there are different demands for different age groups.)


6.  Would your teaching style suit children with special needs? (Teaching children with special needs may mean specific training or hiring specialist staff.)


7.  Are you passionate about, interested in, or merely curious about starting your own art enterprise? How would you rate your desire on a scale from one to ten?


8.  Number the following in order of importance to you when you are considering starting a new venture (1 is most important; 6 is least important):
    _____   Money
    _____   Recognition
    _____   Control of my own working business environment
    _____   Freedom to work as many or as few hours a week, a month, a year, or seasonally
    _____   Time to spend with my family
    _____   Create my own art

9. Why do you want to start your own business? List all the reasons.


10. How many other projects have you started and how committed to them were you?


    a) What were your objectives?


    b) What kind of time lines did you establish to complete individual objectives?


    c) Did you finish the projects and what where the outcomes? (Include jobs or enterprises you undertook as an adolescent.)


    d) What lessons did you learn that you can apply to this new venture?


11. Have you researched the feasibility and profitability of your prepared venture? Has your research been in-depth or superficial?


12. Who else will be affected by and/or involved in this business? How will these people be affected and/or involved? (Check the appropriate answers or add to the list.)
    [   ]   Financially
    [   ]   Emotionally and by serving as other means support
    [   ]   Intellectually, through coaching and imparting business know-how
    [   ]   Physically, by running the household while I run the business
    [   ]   Other: _____

13. What is the minimum amount of money that you need to earn in a week, month, or year?


14. Have you put aside enough money for start-up costs and to cover your expenses until your business starts making money?


15. What are you willing or able to put up as collateral if you need to borrow money (e.g., to rent a retail space)?

16. How often do you intend to run the classes? (Check all answers that apply.)
    [   ]   Summertime only
    [   ]   Once a week
    [   ]   Monday through Friday
    [   ]   Weekends only
    [   ]   Go with the demand and expand as I go
    [   ]   Other: _____

17. What are your short- (first year), medium- (two to three years), and long-term (three to five years) goals?


18. To meet your goals, how much time per week or per month are you willing and able to commit to the success of your new endeavor?


19. How many hours in a week, month, or year will you spend on each of the following?
    [   ]   Strategizing _____
    [   ]   Implementing market research _____
    [   ]   Creating and distributing leaflets and newsletters _____
    [   ]   Cultivating contacts and networking _____
    [   ]   Preparing and planning classes, birthday parties, and other services _____
    [   ]   Calling prospective clients and contacts _____

20. What will you do if there is not enough interest in your services during the first few weeks or months of running your business? (Check all answers that apply.)
    [   ]   Capitulate, close down, and try something completely different
    [   ]   Reevaluate my marketing strategies
    [   ]   Ask for feedback from current students about what is working and what can be improved
    [   ]   Increase the advertising budget and raise the school's profile.

## Taking Stock of Your Answers

Did your answers reveal that you have a passion for teaching art? Or are you better suited to hold the supervisory and administrative reins rather than doing the hands-on teaching?

Start by being honest with yourself about your challenges and successes. If you have enough experience and energy to get this venture off the ground, start by conceptualizing your ideas and then compile a thorough business plan. (For more information on preparing your business plan, see Chapter 5.)

Some spouses are proud to share in the journey of their significant others, while others feel threatened. If you have any doubt about the stability of your relationship while building your business, then talk the situation over very carefully with your spouse and family. You will need to reassure all family members about what it will mean in the short, medium, and long term. Have realistic expectations of them and of yourself and paint the best- and worst-case scenarios for them. Tell them how much it means to you to be doing this and explain why.

If you come up against unrelenting opposition but are determined to go ahead with your plans, consider whether or not you are prepared to risk your marriage and alienate your family. If they need time to adjust to the new ideas, give them some time after which you can discuss and revisit your plan.

# 3

# ORGANIZING YOUR CLASSES

*To give body and perfect form to your thought, this alone is what it is to be an artist.*

— JACQUES-LOUIS DAVID

This chapter is dedicated to how to design and develop your classes and programs. You may already have an idea of what kind of students and classes you want to teach, but be aware that there are many ways to go about it and specific markets you may not know about. This chapter also covers the creative opportunities that await you should you expand your services, including working with children with special needs.

## Finding Inspiration for Your Services

You will need to come up with custom-tailored programs unlike any offered in your vicinity. Think original, fun, and innovative!

## Visit the competition

Check out what programs the competing art schools in your area are offering. Go on the Internet and check out their websites, or visit them in person. Take notes, gather brochures, and complete Exercise 12. Be discreet. You may be tempted to borrow ideas and imitate other businesses you admire, but remember, imitation is not the sincerest form of flattery — it is liable to get you into trouble. No one wants to be copied. Keep high standards of integrity. If you are as resourceful and creative as you can be, you can inject your own individual slant and make the ordinary become extraordinary.

You are getting a feel for what is available and figuring out what you would like

## EXERCISE 12
## RESEARCHING YOUR COMPETITION

1. What do other art schools offer?

2. Do the other schools offer classes for beginners, intermediate students, and portfolio preparation?

3. Do these schools have packages for birthday parties, seasonal camps, and special occasion events?

4. What do you like about these other schools?

5. How would you do things differently in your business?

to do differently and better than the rest. Think about how you can improve upon other schools' ideas. You want to give your clients a high caliber of service but you can only attract new clients by keeping things fresh and vibrant.

## Arts and crafts stores

Visit your local arts and crafts supply store. This really is a great resource. Browse around. You will find a full range of invaluable project and lesson ideas, books, art supplies, and age-appropriate kits. For example, while searching for supplies — and inspiration — for a summer camp program, I came across "memory wire" in the beads aisle of Michaels (the arts and crafts store). I discovered that this wire could easily be fashioned into a necklace (from the large loops) and a bracelet (from the small loops). I could see that this had a "wow" factor, for any age group. And I was right. That summer my female students unanimously agreed that the jewelry-making project was a great success (and the end-of-camp survey proved it). You can never give your students too much new and stimulating enjoyment!

## Take an Artist's Day

It is vital that you surround yourself with stimuli that will replenish your own well of creativity so you can cultivate and inspire that creativity in your students and staff. Make an appointment with yourself to regularly go on what some artists, writers, and motivational speakers call an "Artist's Day." On this day you do nothing but feed the creative, inventive part of yourself. Go to an art gallery or exhibition to simply enjoy the artwork, or bask in the sunshine on a park bench and wallow in nature and its beauty.

Make a promise to yourself to take an Artist's Day once or twice a month and stick to it.

## Other areas of inspiration

You can be inspired by many things: classical art, contemporary art, and in fact any image, photographed or illustrated, and anything you see in the world around you. The following is a more specific list of inspirations, which you may end up using in your art classes:

- Landscapes and seascapes
- Wildlife
- Portraiture and self-portraits
- Still life (a few pieces related or unrelated put in an interesting composition)
- Abstract collages
- Travel, decorating, or gardening magazines
- *National Geographic* magazine
- Postcards
- Art books
- Documentaries on art (on DVD)

An art book that has inspired me over the years is Lin Wellford's *The Art of Painting Animals on Rocks*. I highly recommend this fun and imaginative book. The CD-ROM has an example of her work, as well as photos of rock turtles that my students made at one of my summer camps.

You'll find that there is quite a range of things that inspire you and your students. Ask them what inspires them and incorporate their ideas into your lessons.

## Number of Students per Class and Student/Teacher Ratio

How many students per class should you have? The decision lies in the teacher's expertise and the students' ages and levels of experience. The ideal ratio is one teacher to four students. Even if space allows for many more students at a time, when it comes to younger students I would discourage any more than ten. Always discuss with the assigned teacher how many students he or she is comfortable with.

Assistants can be invaluable in helping with activities or keeping a watchful eye, especially when it comes to outdoor playtime at summer camps. An assistant can also help by setting up, bringing extra materials from storage areas, assisting with cleanup, and generally being a second pair of hands. This leaves the teacher to concentrate on teaching.

If you have an assistant, the ideal student/teacher ratio can be higher, say, six to eight students per class. However, in a less structured class with older artists, such as older students preparing their portfolios, you can easily have ten or more students. Older students may need less hands-on supervision. And some may become assistants for your younger students, especially since studious teenage artists often act as role models for younger children.

Communicate with your students and do not underestimate their input and preferences. Discuss their progress and get feedback from their parents.

## Dividing Your Classes by Age

One of the most important questions to ask yourself is whether you prefer to teach children or adults. Or do you plan to teach both children and adults? Consider the following questions:

- Do you enjoy spending your time and energy creating art with, or imparting your knowledge to, your friends?

- Do you naturally thrive in the company of children? And do they gravitate toward you?

- How confident are you in your abilities as a teacher to inspire and instruct adults, considering the range of artistic ability and learning styles?

### Younger age groups

Younger children can be divided into two categories: five- to seven-year-olds and eight- to ten-year-olds.

The way children learn and what they learn have a direct impact on their well-being and self-image later on. Young children have little fear of failure, and they tend not to suffer the constraints of self-criticism. They pick up multiple languages with ease and creative ideas flow freely from them. They learn an amazing array of activities that are new and unfamiliar to their young minds, absorbing everything like a sponge. Gaining motor skills and physical expertise in a relatively short time depends mainly on the level of curiosity (of which they have an abundance) and the stimulus around them. Their sense of right and wrong, and of their own likes and dislikes are formed quite early in their first years of development.

You may find yourself in a situation where one of your students is too young, too immature for his or her age, or obviously does not want to be there. This can be very disruptive. If it becomes evident that the parent has not told you the whole truth about a child's level of maturity, and the child's behavior unsettles the class, take immediate action. You may even have to call the child's parent to collect the child in the middle of a lesson and offer to discuss the situation later.

Often younger children, or those with autism, take longer to adjust to a new environment. For example, at Jolly Good Art, a mother brought in her daughter for a trial session, joining five other new beginners. Within the first ten minutes the bubbly, sweet, and enthusiastic child was proving to be too distracting for the class with her constant talking and interruptions. Her mother had been asked to stay in the sitting room area in case she was needed and, in this case, she was. (Usually if the child knows his or her parent is near, it helps him or her settle into a new routine.)

You will need to be diplomatic and discreet when discussing the problems a child is creating in a class. Parents can become defensive when there is anything negative mentioned about their child, so you need to give positive options to the situation. The strategy I used with this child was to explain to the parent that her daughter might be better off having some private one-on-one classes. I suggested that the child was not quite ready for the class environment and that after some private lessons the parent could check the child's progress (for example, by letting him or her participate in charity events with other children). I believe this was the best way forward for everyone concerned. With experience and patience, you can learn to meet everyone's needs. Even if you do not want to lose a potential student, this may happen occasionally. There may be students who complain to their parents of unequal attention, and you may have those children vote with their feet and not return.

Be aware that younger children have a shorter attention span. Your lesson plans should concentrate on developing artistic skills but should always encourage fun. Be vigilant for any signs that your students are feeling overwhelmed or are trying too hard to please you or their parents, as this could lead to other problems. You do not want any child to feel the need to perform or keep up with their peers. Focus on sparking their creativity and they will flourish.

## Classes for teenagers and pre-teens

Classes for teenagers and pre-teens can target students ranging in age from 11 to 14 years, or from 15 to 18 years or older. These age groups are great as you can involve students in the decision making and planning of field trips and courses of study. Remember to stay on topic, however, whether for a class or a trip — kids this age appreciate focus and direction. This is also a wonderful age group to take to art museums and art galleries. Have the class draw classic sculptures or study and emulate the color, perspective, light, and shade used by famous artists.

There are many projects you can do that teenagers will find fun and exciting. For example, have them create large portraits of each other or themselves with the help of a mirror, using any type of media. (See two examples of this on the CD.) They could also try figure drawing using a model or just someone in the class.

Still life can also make for an interesting project. Have students paint or draw fruit, reflective objects, crockery, textiles, or a pair of shoes. Encourage students to bring interesting objects — even pictures can be part of a still life.

Some ideas for field trips include going to a dance, martial arts, or yoga studio, or to an equestrian school. Drawing people or animals in motion is a great experience as students work fast to try and capture movement. Armed with portable chairs, sketching pads, and pencils, the students can explore nature firsthand. Have them concentrate on the highlights and shadows of muscles, on light and tone, and on scale.

You can also get them to explore perspectives at a park or at a museum or art gallery. They could create their drawings using buildings, structures, arbors, or sculptures as inspiration.

Note that for minors (students younger than 18), you will need to get the permission of their parents for the students to go on the field trip. Form 1 (also on the CD-ROM) is an example of what you should include in your permission form.

## Overlapping ages

You may find that some students pick up techniques as naturally as a duck takes to water — talent and interest make for fast learners. Some students may have more experience, from having gone to another school or having had artistic parents at home. These people may fit better in the next class up, regardless of age. Gauge suitability and comprehension levels during the first consultation. Monitor progress. Being placed in the right class will keep students stimulated. You do not want them to get bored or de-motivated by covering ground they have already explored.

Be discreet, fair, and diplomatic. You do not want to antagonize other students, or other parents who believe *their* children should be "moved up" a level. Clarify the importance of not rushing or pressuring students unnecessarily, and of building a strong foundation. Ideally, you want your clients to respect and value your expertise, and for all students to flourish and be inspired under your mentorship.

## Adult classes

One of the advantages of teaching adults is that they are more likely to be available during the hours when children are at school. They will also enjoy the chance to rediscover and/or hone their artistic talents and to use their imagination. If your studio is located in a residential area, with families and schools, you should think about targeting this market.

It is very important to determine the preferences and skill levels of your adult students. Beginners would appreciate step-by-step help; others may want something less structured, perhaps mere supervision of independent projects.

# FORM 1
# RELEASE FORM FOR FIELD TRIPS

_____ *(name of school)* is taking a field trip to

_____on _____ *(date and time)*.

The purpose of this event is _____
*(e.g., to visit a new art exhibit or for students to draw in the park)*.

Meals will/will not *(circle appropriate answer)* be provided.

The student will need to bring _____ *(e.g., art materials,*
*weather-appropriate clothing, money, etc.)*.

The cost of the field trip is $_____, which will cover the following expenses:
_____ *(e.g., gas, bus rental, entry fees, etc.)*.

By signing this form, you, the parent or guardian, understand that the student's participation in
the field trip involves risk not found in the normal classroom environment. This includes risks
involved with traveling to and returning from the location. Every safety precaution will be taken
by _____ *(name of school)* to protect your child's
welfare during the field trip.

Please check all boxes that apply and complete the following information:

[    ] I give permission for my child, _____, to attend
the field trip on _____.

[    ] I will take my child to _____ *(name of school)* at
_____ *(time)*, and I give permission for my child to ride in a car or
bus with an instructor or parent.

[    ] I give permission for my child to be taken home after the field trip has ended.

[    ] I will pick up my child from _____ *(name of place)* at
_____ *(time)*.

[    ] I would like to volunteer as a chaperone.

[    ] As a chaperone, I can provide transportation for students.

Please have your child return this form by _____ *(date)* if you are giving
him or her permission to go on the field trip.

By signing and returning this form to the teacher you are giving your child permission to go
on the field trip.

Parent or Guardian's signature: _____

Parent or Guardian's name *(print name)*: _____

Emergency contact phone number: _____

Date: _____

Community centers and senior residential homes are great places where you can offer to set up painting or drawing classes — or classes in glass painting, mosaics, or whatever your specialty or whatever the market demands.

## Portfolio Preparation

Whether it is one of your students trying to get work in a specialized field, or applying to an art college or some other arts institution, he or she must prepare a set of diverse art pieces, perhaps using a variety of media, and put it all in a presentation case: a portfolio. The portfolio is used in interviews for college placements or for getting work, and is an important means of showcasing one's best work, capabilities, and perhaps progress over time.

Be up to date with the art curricula of the colleges your students are interested in. There can be a wide range of specialties. Keep up with the trends, attend college open days, and study college websites. If you build a rapport with college staff, perhaps they can help you customize your courses so you can better prepare your students.

You may offer a course specifically designed for portfolio preparation. Let students work at their own pace on their own projects, but keep a close eye on the time line. Make sure your students are aware of what has to be accomplished during the course, of how to manage their time, and of how to gauge their own progress. Make them accountable. We all need to learn time management and self-discipline, and the earlier this is learned the easier it will be later in life.

## Private Art Classes

You may decide to offer private, one-on-one classes for any number of reasons. As mentioned earlier, some students such as those with special needs will do better if they start off in a private class and then eventually graduate to a group setting, as this will slowly improve their self-confidence.

Private classes can also be helpful for those who need to work on a big project in a short space of time. This can happen when students realize that a big interview date for a college or job is suddenly looming and they do not feel prepared enough.

## Parent-and-Child Classes

Having a combined class of children and their parents can bring family members closer together. They get to spend quality time together, doing something relaxed, fun, and creative. Give them freedom to choose their own projects, and to decide how they want to go about them. Would they like to work together from the same still life? For you, the most important thing to remember is to keep the ambiance informal so they can loosen up and be creative together.

I started these combined classes at Jolly Good Art when a father of a special needs child wanted to spend more time with his son. As time went by, the father became more and more excited about his own artistic talent, just as much as his son's improved artwork.

I also taught a teenage daughter and a mother who used the classes to bridge the gap between them. The studio was an artistic space for them where they could relax. (I have paintings and books lining the walls, and music playing — jazz, classical, or whatever my clients prefer.) Their common ground was fashion, and I had them contribute to one still life project with their own costume jewelry, shoes, and clothing with interesting fabrics.

# Teaching Students with Special Needs

If you want to teach students with special needs, you will need to learn about the various challenges you may come across and to understand the breadth of disorders and specific needs. You may already have specialist training or have transferable skills from your past experiences, or you may plan to pursue more formal training, such as in art therapy. Remember, the goal of the art teacher is to help the student to develop and evolve using self-expression through art.

What kind of special needs students will you teach and how are you going to go about it? There are three areas of special needs that I came across at Jolly Good Art, and different teaching approaches need to be considered for each. A student may be diagnosed with a high-functioning or severe level of autism and experience challenges when it comes to language and social interaction. For a student with cerebral palsy, you will also have to consider his or her level of dexterity and hand-eye coordination, which may hinder him or her from progressing as quickly as another child with more autonomous control. And for a student diagnosed with Attention Deficit Hyperactivity Disorder (ADHD) and similar syndromes, you will need to determine how easily he or she is distracted in order to create an appropriate program.

---

Although Traci Tomkin, who owns a pottery school called Throwing a Fit, did not initially think of teaching children, it seemed a natural fit. Traci had anticipated teaching adults, perhaps giving parents or caregivers a bit of a break from their responsibilities, but there was an obvious need for children — and children with special needs — to take part in their own play with clay. So, being an adaptable entrepreneur, she gave her customers what they needed.

"I enjoyed their creativity, their excitement with the feeling of the clay. Children have a fearlessness; they are open to exploring their ideas using my suggestions and willing to try new things."

Traci has a professional background and is a mother of two children with special needs. Her tagline is "Beat Stress, Play with Clay." If her students with special needs sometimes do not feel like following class instructions, she lets them smash clay on a board. "They really enjoy this. It allows them to get physical without hurting anyone, and it gets rid of their frustrations."

---

Once you have assessed the child's dexterity, hand-eye coordination, and level of concentration, offer the parent the option of paying per class rather than for an entire course. This will allow both you and the parent to decide whether the classes are working out. Monitor the child's progress and communicate frequently with his or her parents. You can ascertain the student's interest level and vary the lessons accordingly, even changing the subject halfway through if the student shows any signs of impatience, boredom, or distress.

In all cases make sure you understand what the parents want and need from you. Be prepared for unusual demands, and always make any suggestions that may benefit their child.

You may also need to make your studio wheelchair accessible. This may include adding ramps to the entry and having wider doorways so that the wheelchairs can get into the class. For one of my students I custom-made an "art chair" with cushions in which his parent would carry him into the studio.

At Jolly Good Art I saw, time and time again, just how patience and understanding reap rewards for everyone. Creating art can give one an immeasurable sense of accomplishment. There is nothing more heartwarming than seeing that bright smile on a student's face when receiving an art award for spectacular achievement.

Throughout the years I have had the privilege of working with many young artists with an extraordinary drive and sense of fun despite their physical or mental challenges. Witnessing determination through adversity can be inspiring. My daughter sometimes joined the classes, and I witnessed a new sense of maturity in her.

## Cerebral palsy

Zak, a bright, sociable ten-year-old boy who was in a wheelchair due to cerebral palsy,

was brought to Jolly Good Art by his father so they could spend their Wednesday afternoons together creating art. Zak was obviously very interested in art, but he seemed hesitant in the beginning, unsure he could master the class projects. The restrictive use of his hands made it difficult for him to hold an oil pastel stick unless it was a thick one. But he listened attentively and made the effort to do his very best, and, with every passing week, he gained self-confidence and kept improving.

Within a couple of months this student was flourishing. His always-positive attitude — even when working with oil pastels and some other tools that proved too arduous — meant he would always try and improve. His forte was his light touch with watercolors; after only a few lessons he showed an uncanny knack for this medium. Whether it was also with acrylic or gouache, he seemed to know color and how and when to apply the next coat of paint. (See the CD-ROM for pictures of two of his paintings.)

The materials and media you get your students to use depend on their level of dexterity and their preference. Try out a range of tools in the beginning. Large oil and chalk pastels, acrylics, and watercolors tend to work best.

## Autism

If a child diagnosed with autism wants to take lessons in your studio, do not eliminate the possibility just because you do not have trained staff. Offer a half-hour consultation and determine the student's comprehension levels and communication abilities. Is the child diagnosed with high-functioning autism or high-level autism? But remember, more important than medical diagnosis is what the child shows an aptitude for. During a consultation at Jolly Good Art the teacher would sit next to the student and get him or her to study a still life or photograph, and to draw it in a sketchpad.

The most important thing to remember here is the communication the teacher can attain with the student. Severely autistic students need to be brought back from their own little world with a lot of direction.

The media I suggested in the last section on cerebral palsy are also suitable for children with autism. But it may take a bit of time to suss out what the child likes to work with, and what subject will work best. In some cases a choice of what to paint or draw may confuse the student. The teacher may have to slowly introduce art materials and subjects that may not be the student's first choice. At first, classes should never last longer than an hour. The lesson time can slowly increase as you gauge the student's level of concentration. Ask the parent to stay in the waiting room to help make the child feel more comfortable.

At Jolly Good Art there was a student that was diagnosed with Asperger's syndrome, which is sometimes defined as a form of high-functioning autism. He was easily distracted in class, but he displayed great passion for drawing anything and everything to do with lions. Within a few weeks the student had been weaned off of just drawing lions and was expected to draw and paint other things.

He was given a choice of wildlife pictures (other than lions). He was taught to look at the shapes and lines, the highlights and shadows. At home he could choose to draw anything at all, from his imagination or from books. The teacher would look at these at the next lesson and make encouraging and constructive comments and ask him questions about it, including what the boy had learned in the process.

Although his favorite animal was still the lion, within a few short months the student was drawing everything from buildings to cars, farm animals, seascapes, and landscapes, and in the various media he had shied away from in the beginning. He accomplished a lot, both at Jolly Good Art and at school. It was a joy to see his proud smile when he saw his paintings on the Jolly Good Art website. He also started winning prizes for his art. His drawing of a Bengal tiger was published in an Autism Society book of art.

Please refer to the web resources section on the CD-ROM for more information about autism.

## Attention Deficit Hyperactivity Disorder (ADHD)

For the child with Attention Deficit Hyperactivity Disorder (ADHD) or other similar conditions, art classes can be one way to improve the child's focus and concentration. Ask the parent about the child's artistic endeavors and interests and other extracurricular activities, and the parent's desires for the child. Your role is to enhance the child's overall growth through artistic self-expression.

Offer a trial lesson to estimate the child's interest and concentration level. Decide whether it is better to go at a slower pace in a private class, rather than in a group class which may be too distracting. If you honestly believe the child will not progress under your tutelage, explain your reasons to the parent. You may suggest other places that specialize in teaching children with ADHD. Provide contacts that you should have through your network.

## Art therapy

There are many definitions of art therapy. Generally, it is used in conjunction with psychotherapy, to increase and maintain emotional well-being. From my experience, parents who seek art therapy for their children want their children to learn to express their feelings through art, to enhance their language skills, and to better comprehend the world around them. Even without specialized training in art therapy, you may still be requested to offer your services.

Build a network and rapport with local art therapists who you can recommend should your services be unable to meet the particular needs of parents. Their personal physicians should also be able to provide references. (For more information about art therapy, visit the American Art Therapy Association's website at www.arttherapy.org.)

## Seasonal Programs

After the first few months of classes it seemed a natural progression for Jolly Good Art to offer summer camp programs, especially since so many parents were asking about it. You may also find demand for Christmas and spring break programs, even for just a craft day or two. (See the section Special Occasion Parties later in this chapter.)

Complete Exercise 13 to find out if you are ready to run a seasonal program. Think about when and how long your seasonal camp is going to be. The summer camps at Jolly Good Art were first offered as half-day camps, from 9:45 a.m. to 1:00 p.m., from the beginning of July through to part of August. But because of popular demand, the following year we also included full-day camps that went to 3:30 p.m. As the momentum grew, I employed more teachers and assistants. Some students signed up for only one week, some students signed up for a month, and some signed up for the entire summer. You may decide to run your summer camp to the very end of August.

There are many aspects to seasonal camps, not only in terms of the variety of projects. You must ensure a constant supply of art materials as well as food, and perhaps organize games and water play (in the summertime) as a break. Communication between you and the staff is key.

Camps are a little different from classes you would offer during the year, which are more structured with a narrower age range. Camps, on the other hand, are geared to be more fluid and "fun-filled," and for a variety of ages. (I must mention that learning new art skills still plays a huge part at a camp.) This gets to be a bit tricky, as your students will be at different levels. Are you going to have your students work on the same project or different projects? Should you separate them into groups? I find myself separating students according to their level of experience, rather than by age.

Keep in mind that siblings, cousins, and friends may all sign up for the same summer camp, so if they are especially young they may distract each other if seated at the same table. Discreetly move them to separate tables with a promise they'll be reunited at the break.

# EXERCISE 13
# SEASONAL PROGRAMS

Consider the following questions if you are deciding whether or not to offer seasonal programs:

1.  How many weeks of the summer will you dedicate to a summer camp?

2.  How many students will you cater to on a weekly basis?

3.  For what age ranges and experience levels will the camp be?

4.  Will you be running the program yourself with assistants or will you supervise the program and employ teachers to instruct?

5.  Will you need to make arrangements for your own children if you offer a camp during their vacation time?

6.  When can you schedule time for yourself and your family?

As an art teacher, you may be exposing students — and maybe their friends, siblings, and cousins — to a new world of art. And as a camp director, you are seeking to provide optimum enjoyment and unique memorable experiences.

Do not forget your family throughout all this. Do not sacrifice your family time in the weeks, months, and years of your business. The days are long, but the years zoom by pretty fast. And mixing business with family is not always a good solution. I did not give in to the temptation to let my young daughter attend my first summer camp program. To put it bluntly, in a classroom situation it may be possible that people appear much more patient with and considerate of their students than with their own offspring!

I also didn't sacrifice holidays. I personally made sure to take time off with the family before my summer camp would start, even if it was just to the nearest beach, or a short weekend away to Niagara Falls. I also sometimes took a short break in between camps, or a full week or more at the end of August.

See Form 2 for a Registration Form, and Form 3 for a Summer Camp Confirmation sheet for parents. It is a useful reminder of the address of the summer camp, when it starts, and what the camper should bring.

## Projects for seasonal camps

In addition to the usual materials, you can provide more craft and "fiddly" items suitable for summer camps, such as rock painting. Be aware that some projects are more time-consuming than others, some taking up an entire day, a week, or longer. For example,

mosaics and rock painting can take a lot of preparation, drying, and curing time between each phase. You must design your program so that there is plenty of time for everyone to finish their projects.

For a mosaic tile project, you would first describe and show the materials to be used, the steps to be taken, and the end result. Safety is important here, and you would provide gloves, towels, and goggles for the "smashing" process. All children love to shatter the multicolored tiles, after which they put the broken pieces into separate clear jars. The next stage is for the students to find a picture or come up with an imaginary design and transfer it to high-density fiberboard (hardboard) or medium-density fiberboard (MDF). Next you would talk to students about different types of glues and their quick-drying tendencies. Watch over the students' progress without interfering. The older students and those who are staying longer can take on a more intricate project.

Do not let the younger ones get overwhelmed or compare themselves to others. Keep an eye on their progress and confirm they do not need to prove anything to the teacher, their siblings, or their peers.

There are many activities that may look intimidating to some students, especially if those students are new to your camp or to art in general. With your expertise you will be able to gauge when their comfort level increases. Reassure them. Ask the other regular students to share their experiences with similar media and subjects.

Come up with your own programs with your own unique twists. If you see a good picture of a sunset but do not like all the

# FORM 2
# REGISTRATION FORM

You will receive an early bird discount of 10 percent if you register before
_____. Bring a friend to join in the fun!

Parent's name: _____

Student's name: _____

Student's age: _____

Address: _____

_____

Home telephone: _____

Work telephone: _____

Cell phone: _____

Email: _____

Health issues: _____

_____

Allergies (List all known allergies to food, medicines, and art materials
such as latex gloves): _____

_____

_____

How did you hear about _____ *(name of business)*?

Regular Class Registration:
*(List classes provided and cost)*

Seasonal Camp Registration:

Preferred weeks of attendance: _____
    [   ] Half day
    [   ] Full day

$_____ for half-day weeks x number of weeks _____ = Total $ _____

$_____ for full-day weeks x number of weeks _____ = Total $ _____

Payment:
    [   ] Check
    [   ] Cash
    [   ] Credit card _____ *(type of card; e.g., Visa, MasterCard)*
             _____ *(card number)* _____ *(expiry date)*
    [   ] Other: _____

# FORM 3
## SUMMER CAMP CONFIRMATION

Thank you for choosing to spend part of your summer holidays at
_____ *(name of art school)*.

We are going to have a GREAT time with lots of creative ART and lots of FUN in the SUN
— so don't forget to bring your sunscreen, hats, and swimsuits!

Description of the program (including the lunch menu) will be available on the
_____ page on the website _____ *(URL)*
on _____ *(date)*. Thank you for your continued commitment to art, and
we are looking forward to seeing you on _____ *(date of program start)*.

In the meantime, if you have any questions, please call _____ *(phone
number)*.

We are looking forward to creating and enjoying art with you this summer!


_____

*(name of owner and/or school)*


_____
_____
_____

*(address of venue)*

colors in it, you can of course use your artistic license to make it your own. And study children closely. Watch them create their own masterpieces. What do they like to do again and again without getting bored? Ask them what they enjoy doing and why they enjoy doing it.

## Food for summer campers

Do you like to cook? Do you have the space, time, or the inclination to prepare snacks for a summer camp? And for camps that last a full day, will you provide lunch or have students bring their own?

In addition to healthy snacks, fruits, and drinks, Jolly Good Art served lots of water throughout the day. The full-day campers were also offered lunches, or the students could bring their own (should they have allergies for example). The group lunch was one of the highlights of the summer camp, especially the Fridays, which were "pizza and ice cream cones" days. Since the end of a weekly, biweekly, or monthly camp would fall on a Friday, pizza day would always mark a special occasion.

As a mother, I considered what lunches and snacks would meet the "healthy, fun, and delicious" criteria. Children certainly know what they like and do not like. But I noticed that they are more willing to try eating something new when they are in a new environment that is fun. They are meeting new friends, trying out new projects, and excelling on new levels; they are exploring.

I did stick to the classics that almost all children enjoy. Ask questions to find out what food is the most popular. And get the students to help decide on the menu. This validates their opinions, and gets them involved. (For an example of an easy-to-make treat, see the Yummy Chocolate Brownies Recipe on the CD-ROM.)

The menu for the full-day campers was chosen with great care, taking into account all the children's input. At the end of the program I asked students to complete questionnaires about what they liked and disliked about the seasonal camp, including the food. I incorporated some of the students' suggestions into the following year's programs and menus. See Form 4.

---

### Sample Menu

**Snacks**

- Fruit
- Cereal bars
- Popcorn
- Cheese and crackers
- Pita and hummus
- Tortilla chips and salsa
- Ice cream and Popsicles

**Lunches**

- Toasted cheese sandwiches and veggie sticks (e.g., carrot, celery, bell pepper, cucumber)
- Hot dogs — chicken, veggie, or beef (all kosher)
- Macaroni and cheese with bread crumbs or cheese crust
- Tuna or egg salad sandwiches
- Pizza

---

# FORM 4
## SEASONAL CAMP SURVEY

A quick survey to find out how the _____
*(name of art school camp)* was for you.

Name: _____    Age: _____

1. Is this the first time you have been to the camp?


2. How much did you enjoy the different camp activities? Put an X in the appropriate box:

| Activity | I did not like it | I liked it a bit | I liked it | I loved it |
|---|---|---|---|---|
| Oil pastels | | | | |
| Glass painting | | | | |
| Watercolors | | | | |
| Rock art | | | | |
| Mosaic art | | | | |
| Acrylic art | | | | |
| Fabric painting | | | | |
| Breaks/water play | | | | |
| Yoga | | | | |
| Other: | | | | |

3. Which snacks did you enjoy? What was your favorite snack? Put an X in the appropriate box:

| Snack | I did not like it | I liked it | I loved it |
|---|---|---|---|
| Fruit | | | |
| Cereal bars | | | |
| Drinks | | | |
| Popcorn | | | |
| Cheese | | | |
| Crackers | | | |
| Pita and hummus | | | |
| Salsa and chips | | | |
| Ice cream | | | |
| Freezies | | | |
| Pizza | | | |
| Other: | | | |

4. Can you suggest any other snacks you would like to have at future camps?

5. What art project would you like to try again?

6. What subjects and materials would you like to try?

7. What was your favorite break activity?

8. Would you come back next summer and why?

9. Would you like to take art lessons and learn more?

### Food allergies

Allergies of any kind should be taken very seriously. You want your students to be as safe as possible. Students with extreme allergies usually bring their own lunches.

Pay careful attention to all allergies the parents report on the registration forms. (See Form 2, the Registration Form.) This includes not only food allergies, but allergies to certain nonprescription drugs and to art materials such as latex gloves. You should also know what medications are necessary if the child does encounter an allergic reaction.

Are you or is your staff willing to take responsibility for a child with allergies? You may need to carry an EpiPen (a device that injects a single dose of epinephrine) or have other medication on hand in case of an emergency. Consider the pros and cons because this is a big responsibility. There have been cases when I have refused to take an acutely allergic child.

# Special Occasion Parties

Special occasion parties for Mother's and Father's Day weekends, birthdays, and the end of the school year are all fun opportunities for creative time with special projects that children can take home. Here even siblings with a four-year age gap (e.g., 8- and 12-year-olds) can comfortably work on the same projects.

As with any kind of class, what projects you give your students can depend on the time of year and what students have enjoyed doing in the past. You figure this out not only by conducting surveys, but also through experience. There will be fun,

failure-proof activities that may become your school's trademark.

# Birthdays

Make each birthday party unique and memorable for the child. Have the child and the parent choose the art project. Make sure it is simple but fun, and easy to clean up. Remember, the party may sometimes be held at the child's home and the parents will not want to clean up paint from the carpets!

At Jolly Good Art I created all the birthday party invitations but the parent and child made all the decisions about what the invitation should say and where the party would take place (see Form 5). The parents distributed the invites to the guests. Mostly the party was held at the studio, and other times at their home or someplace else.

I customized the invitations, at times incorporating a special picture or photo of something that the birthday child particularly liked, or a reproduction of the child's own painting. Sometimes I would include computer-generated images ranging from a mermaid or ballet shoes, to something sports related. Full details about the party and a map for directions were included on the back of the invitation.

I always assembled personalized gift bags to give to the children at the end of the party. These were greatly appreciated. I added unique touches — for example, candy kebabs, or colorful Mini Eggs for a March or April birthday party. And I paid special attention to the gift bag wrapping. (See a photo of a gift bag on the CD-ROM.)

Every guest received a thank-you note from the birthday child in the gift bags.

# FORM 5
# BIRTHDAY PARTY PLANNING

Birthday child's name and age: _____

Date of party: _____

Address: _____

Phone number: _____ Number of guests: _____

1. **Project chosen** (e.g., glass painting, oil pastel, watercolor):

   _____

2. **Materials required** (e.g., glass or Perspex frame for glass painting):

   _____

3. **Invitations**

   Choice of front picture (e.g., student's painting, computer-generated, or other idea):

   _____

   Text inside card: _____

   _____

4. **Snacks/Meals**

   What does the child prefer for snacks?

   _____

   What does the child prefer for the meal?

   _____

   What kind of drinks will be served?

   _____

   What kind of dessert will be served?

   _____

   Does anyone attending have food allergies?

   _____

   Does the meal need to be kosher?

   _____

   By what time should the meal be ready or delivered?

   _____

   What time will the cake be cut?

   _____

   What additional items will be needed (e.g., paper plates, cups, cutlery, table covers)?

   _____

   Will you need balloons and/or banners?

   _____

5. **Do you have other special party instructions?**

   _____

   _____

Information about my studio's services was placed on the back of the thank-you note or included as a leaflet. Not only was this extra advertising for the school, the birthday child's parent did not have to create or buy thank-you cards.

Fees for the parties vary depending on the art activities the clients choose. My package deal fee included everything but the cake (because there are so many types of birthday cakes out there). See the next chapter for Jolly Good pricing.

When organizing birthday parties, make them as personal as possible. All the details count. Word of mouth will follow.

# CLASS PRICES AND MATERIALS

*Money is like a sixth sense without which you cannot make a complete use of the other five.*

— W. SOMERSET MAUGHAM

As important as market research, business planning, and promotion — all of which we will get to later — are your business's pricing strategies. As my friend Heather Skoll says, "When we are so engrossed in creating and sharing our art and programs, it is easy to lose track of time and undercharge ourselves. Or even sometimes not pay ourselves."

## Pricing

Take notice of how much time and energy it takes to run your classes. Exactly how much is spent before, during, and after? This will help you calculate what your time is worth. Take into account your planning and preparation time as well as your expertise. After all, you acknowledge how much your doctor's, car mechanic's, or accountant's time is worth. You must respect your own talents and needs accordingly.

If you are aware of what your time costs you, you can learn to delegate and contract out activities to others. These people may include bookkeepers, accountants, or web designers. These professionals can be worth their fees if you do your homework and communicate with them clearly. This frees up your time to concentrate on the many other aspects of running your business.

When pricing your services, think about the art experience you are offering. How much are you and your unique talents worth? How much are creative exploration, self-discovery, and self-development worth to your clients?

There are many ways to price your services. Start by researching the price structure of other similar schools and camps. Keep your pricing on par with the other schools and educational establishments in your vicinity, and not just in your target area. Note the differences between your school and the competition in terms of the following:

- Student/teacher ratio

- Quality of art supplies and materials

- Art projects

- Depth and quality of services offered

Be realistic but do not underprice your services just because you are starting out and are eager to get new clients, or because you have a home-based studio. You still have expenses that need to be covered. Also remember that when you undersell, it may give the wrong impression that the quality of your services may be substandard.

Use your common sense and your intuition, but also do your homework. Price the various services as competitively as you can afford. And after doing all this homework, you *will* have to start somewhere and set a price. You will soon know how well it is working.

If, despite your market research, you are not getting enough students, then perhaps you have set too high a price for your targeted area. But before coming to the conclusion that it is simply the pricing that needs revising, you may have to ask yourself some tough questions. Are you offering as high a quality of service as you can? Are your classes as inspiring as they could be?

If, on the other hand, you are getting overbooked within the first couple of months, you may indeed be undercharging for your caliber of service.

## Calculating your price

Your price structure also depends on many other factors, including the following:

- Hourly rate

- Staff

- Materials and supplies

- Food or snacks (if included)

- Marketing costs (e.g., leaflets and brochures, mailings, newspaper ads, and business cards)

- Overhead costs (e.g., phone, website, rent, computer, and computer software)

When I first started Jolly Good Art, I charged $125 per student for six-week sessions. The classes totaled 12 hours — a two-hour class per week for six weeks.

Every year I increased the costs by a percentage that reflected the increase in the cost of materials and in the number of staff. I also took into consideration the new projects introduced that year.

For the seasonal camps I gave the clients a choice of half days or full days. The half-day camps were $135 per week, for approximately 16 hours per week. The full-day camps were $230 per week, for approximately 27 hours a week. The price included all materials, food, and drinks, as well as pizza and ice cream on Fridays.

After calculating the cost of art supplies, food, staff, and other items, I realized that I had to have at least six campers a week to make a summer camp profitable. And in the first couple of years I did indeed average to six or seven campers. After that, the average grew to 12 or 13 students every week.

The fees for regular classes and seasonal camps were always paid ahead at registration. I included a 10-percent discount for early registration. This was well received by many students, especially with new campers who also brought their friends and cousins.

For birthday parties I charged $195 for a party of ten children, and I added $20 per additional child. The price of the package increased depending on the chosen activity. For example, an oil pastel project (where pre-cut mats were provided) cost less to organize than glass painting, which required more preparation time and supplies such as glass and frames. In your quote, you should also take into account the costs involved in packaging the finished artwork.

For private classes, including special needs tutoring and help with portfolio preparation, I charged $30 to $45 dollars per hour. The final price sometimes depended on the level of specialized teaching, for example, for special needs.

## Captive product pricing

Some schools charge reasonable rates but with a catch — students have to buy all their art supplies through the art school. Although I do not like this approach, many schools do operate this way, and in fact many clients do not mind.

I do, however, see nothing wrong with selling art supplies and materials (e.g., paints, brushes, drawing pads, canvases, and easels) to your students for their personal use. (And you could probably get a bulk discount.) In any case, if you decide to sell supplies, you will need to register for sales tax (and apply for a sales tax number) as mentioned in Chapter 1. Most states and provinces charge a retail sales tax, levied on all direct sales to the consumer.

You never know — providing these resources to your students may encourage them to create outside of class time.

## Offering discounts

For the first few months, consider offering incentives to bring in as much business as you can handle. For example, offer discounts for early registration and referrals.

As a show of appreciation, I gave a small discount to students who would routinely sign up for summer camp, or want me to organize their birthday parties. I also gave discounts to those who stayed for more than two weeks at summer camp, and to those who gave referrals.

## Last word on pricing: Intangible value

Although art can be considered a luxury, what you are offering is the opportunity for artistic exploration and development. It's all about the intangible. You are ultimately selling a unique creative experience to your clients. Your classes should be fun, enjoyable, and memorable, and the atmosphere, the project, and everything about your school must have a "wow" factor. You are putting a price on an experience that is priceless.

## Materials and Supplies

The quality and range of art supplies and materials can determine how much your students enjoy working with them. Keep your standards high. And be imaginative when looking around the house for possible materials to use for art projects.

## Costs

As start-up, I spent about $300 to $400 for art materials and supplies, having looked for the best deals. As you start out, research the cost of materials and figure out what kinds of projects you are able to afford at the beginning.

### Start-up Costs for Supplies and Materials

| | |
|---|---|
| Paints (in different media), students' brushes, pastels, etc. | $50 |
| Canvases and drawing pads | $80 |
| 3 easels ($30 each) | $90 |
| 2 sturdy tables ($40 each) | $80 |
| 4 plastic foldaway chairs ($10 each) | $40 |
| Art books (five or six books is a good start; note that book clubs such as North Light Book Club offer an introductory discount) | $60 |
| Total | $400 |

As you can see in the example, I spent the minimum capital I could. I only needed to buy four chairs as I had old ones that I had no more use for and did not mind getting paint on. I also encouraged students to bring in their parents' old shirts to wear as smocks, and I collected old magazines, art books, and garden books from thrift shops and charity stores.

I reserved expensive sable watercolor brushes for the advanced students and for demonstrations. I also taught my students how to clean and look after the brushes. The brushes would last longer and the students would understand how important it was to look after tools to get the most out of them.

As I expanded to accommodate more classes, I bought canvas on a roll and cut and stretched my own sizes. Another way to save money is to ask your local art-store owner if they offer a bulk discount.

## Materials for classes

Whether you are starting out or expanding, the following are some of the materials you may want to obtain for your classes if painting and drawing is what your school will offer:

- Oil pastels
- Chalk pastels
- Watercolor paints and pencils
- Watercolor brushes
- Acrylic and gouache paint (water-based paints)
- Crayons
- Silk paints
- Fabric paints and crayons
- Graphite pencils
- Charcoal sticks
- Glass paints (the nontoxic kind)

You may also want to consider clay. Self-drying clay is widely available and is a better value for your time and money because you will not need a kiln. This clay is also very good for painting projects.

Note that soft oil pastels range in quality, with some suitable for amateur students, and others suitable for professional artists. Just remember that the more pigment these pastels have, the better the quality, which makes them more expensive. Chalk pastels are also available, which some students like because the resulting polish is one that cannot be obtained with oil pastels. I personally love both types, depending on the feel and atmosphere I'm trying to create with a piece of art.

## Canvas

It is best to start students with good quality canvas. Try different types to see what you and your students like best. As mentioned earlier, you can buy bulk canvas on rolls for better value. You may want to experiment with stretching your own canvases on ready-made frames.

## Paper

As with canvas, you will want your students to use good quality paper. There are different kinds of paper that can be used for different projects. Depending on the project, you may want to choose paper that is smooth or rough in texture.

If you will be using watercolor, consider starting with 90 lb (thinner) paper or 140 lb (thicker) paper, the latter of which will absorb more water and be more conducive to special effects. I usually give beginner students a student pad that they can use to practice different techniques, such as how to tape the paper onto a flat, smooth board using masking tape. These are worked on one sheet at a time. They can also buy their own watercolor pads, which are more expensive. They come in pads or spiral binders.

Oil pastel paper varies in thickness, quality, and price. Like the quality of sketchpads or watercolor paper, it is a matter of preference. After trying out the different ones on the market you can make a decision on what would best bring out the students' talents.

Colored paper can be used for collages, painting, and drawing. In certain art supply stores these can be bought in bulk in specific colors. I have found construction paper sold in pads for craft purposes to be very versatile. I have used these for oil pastel painting and to teach the students how the background of the paper affects the end result, making it darker or lighter.

## Materials for special effects projects

There may be many objects around your home that you may not have considered using for art projects. The following may be useful items to have in your studio:

- Cotton swabs
- Toothpicks
- Twigs
- Old toothbrushes
- Rocks and sand
- Salt
- Candle wax
- Glue sticks and regular glue
- Construction paper
- Old cards and magazine clippings

Masking fluid, also known as frisket, is a clear solution that protects the paper from watercolors. When dry, you can peel it off to expose the untouched paper underneath. This is used for highlights or small areas that need to be left white. Note that this rubber solution ruins artists' brushes. Apply with cotton swabs, toothpicks, twigs, or old toothbrushes. There are many good art books that will show you tricks like these.

Cold candle wax is good for a "resist" effect. You apply it to the paper like a crayon. Paint doesn't stick to the waxed area so different colors will show through on the paper. Younger children find this fun to work with. (To be safe, I made it a rule never to let young kids handle *warm* wax or hot glue guns.)

Sand or salt can be used for special watercolor effects. The paint dries with the grains, which soaks up the pigment or varies its lightness and intensity. This has a wonderful "wow" factor.

Toothbrushes can create splattering effects using water-based paints such as watercolor, acrylics, or gouache.

As for collages, imagination is the limit! Beads, pearls, old costume jewelry, buttons, glitter, glitter glue, wrappers, scraps of fabric, or tissue paper can be used with paints, crayons, and/or any media the artist wishes to use.

And as mentioned, rocks as small as pebbles or as large as a dinner plate can be painted. (See examples of rock art on the CD-ROM.)

Porcelain paint can be used to paint glazed or unglazed pottery. Unglazed pottery, however, needs to be fired in a kiln. Maybe you know a potter in your network with whom you can work out a trade for use of his or her kiln for free art classes or whatever you both agree on.

You can also do special projects with fabric. If you sew denim bags or pillowcases, the students can create their own stenciled or painted subjects on them. Since sewing is one of my hobbies, I would always prepare denim bags before a summer camp or charity event so students could paint them with vibrantly colored fabric paints. The designs came from the students or they chose designs from art books. (A sample of my collection is listed in the appendix.) They also wrote dates and the school's name, which made sure the occasion was encapsulated.

And finally, students can decorate blank hardcover journals, scrapbooks, and photo albums you provide, using any art materials mentioned earlier.

# 5

# YOUR BUSINESS PLAN

*He fishes well who uses a golden hook.*

— LATIN PROVERB

In this chapter we will cover the definition of a business plan and the variety of business plans that you can create to suit your business. A business plan will help you with your short-term goals of start-up along with your long-term goals of expansion.

## What Is a Business Plan?

My definition of a business plan is a detailed document of "SMART" goals and objectives. SMART stands for the following:

- *Specific*: Be precise about your actions and objectives

- *Measurable*: Quantify your plans

- *Action-based*: Create goals that you can complete

- *Realistic*: Decide what can be done to deliver on your goals

- *Time-based*: Set specific deadlines

The acronym is originally from the corporate world, and can help you define how your business is conceptualized and operated. To start out confidently and to become successful I strongly urge you to invest the time and effort to develop a business plan. With all the considerations discussed in the previous chapters, such as conceptualizing and developing the artistic side of your business, you will also need to create a business plan that will help you strengthen the practical side, your short- and long-term business vision. The business plan will help you know where you are going and how you will get there, and encourage you to answer the following questions:

- What do you want to achieve?

- Why are you the expert to start and run this venture?

- When can you expect to realistically implement your plans?

- Where do you intend to start the business?

- Who is in your network and professional support system?

- How will you implement your goals and actually run your business?

Although you may hesitate to invest all the energy required for a business plan, do not be impatient. You will find this step invaluable in many ways. Taking the time now will save you months of aggravation later. By anticipating and planning for problems ahead of time, you may prevent catastrophes down the road.

Some people choose to expand their horizons too soon, without going through this step. These people may become overwhelmed or baffled as to how to progress, keep up with demand, best use their resources, and plan in the midst of chaos.

Many businesses have failed. These business owners realized too late that if they had concentrated on creating and developing tangible goals at the beginning, they might have avoided the heartache and the losses (not just financially, but emotionally as well). This is business and there is little room for romantic eagerness.

The business plan sets out to demystify any illusions you may have by making you focus on all the intricacies of your vision. It helps you consider opportunities and challenges. It also helps you concentrate on defining your services for the long term and lets you see the bigger picture beyond using quick persuasive tactics to get clients. A business plan may also prepare you for the unexpected because you have thought ahead and strategized your various start-up, expansion, and long-term goals. But also note that it should be a flexible document. It has to be user-friendly, a document you can easily refine over time as you gain experience.

## Types of Business Plans

There are three main types of business plans: *general blueprint, motivational,* and *financial.*

A general blueprint business plan is created for yourself. It lets you see your goals on paper so you can envision where you are going with your venture.

In the beginning I had not even named my business because I had yet to think of it as a "school" or an "art instruction establishment" — my horizons were still narrow. My very first plan was a blueprint only for myself and not to be shared with anyone else. I used it to —

- create my business goals,

- have my plan in writing,

- see if I was on track (by referring to it often), and

- enable me to implement my goals with confidence.

The motivational business plan is an action plan for you and your staff. It can serve as inspiration for your staff as you run the business and as your business grows. In this plan you share your vision and your goals, and then should inspire in your staff a sense of commitment to your establishment. You also show trust and faith in their abilities and in their contributions to the business.

The financial business plan is created to convince the bank or other institutions that give out business loans that you have thought your idea through and are prepared for any likely contingencies. You will need to prove to the institutions that you —

- have a solid knowledge base,

- have hard assets as security,

- are a good risk,

- are totally committed to your proposed business,

- have a market for your services, and

- are here to stay.

In the appendix, you will find some of the books I have found useful and invaluable over the years in regards to business plans. There is a lot of information available, such as on specific business plans for the product and service sectors and for small businesses and corporations. Pick out one business plan you can use as a template, and as your experience grows and your needs evolve, look at more in-depth plans.

## Business Plan Layout

The following sections outline the information you will need to include in your financial business plan. (Note that this may also be used as a guideline for the blueprint and motivational business plans.)

## Summary

Write a simple description outlining the essential facts about what your particular school/business offers. Remember that this is a summary and does not need to be longer than a few paragraphs. Include the location of the business as well as the legal structure (e.g., S corporation or sole proprietorship). Although this goes at the beginning of your business plan, you may want to write it after you have completed the rest of the document because this section is a summary.

In a financial business plan, you will need to include the amount of funds required to start the business and the terms under which those funds will be repaid.

In a motivational business plan, this section will help your staff see what this business is about and help you articulate your vision.

## Your history

You will need to include a brief history of who you are, and what your qualifications are to run this business. You should describe how your past experience and skills make you a good fit for your own business.

You will need to describe your strengths as accurately as possible so that the lending institution realizes that you are a good risk to lend money to and that you are committed to the business. If you have any experience with running a profitable business or you have taught art classes in the past, use these experiences as examples that highlight your transferable skills.

## Description of your business

Describe your business's history and background. Define what your school's activities will be, and its current position within the marketplace where your clients and competitors are. Evaluate and realistically describe your present services and their market viability.

Explain why there is a need for your business and why it will do well in your targeted area. Give an overview of the demand in the market for your unique services, the profitability, and anticipated future growth.

## Operations and management team

Give an overview of the relevant qualifications, backgrounds, and responsibilities of your operations staff and management. For example, describe your assistants, specialist teachers, and the people in your support system. Your support system can include your family, network of business contacts, and coaches or mentors that have influence on the day-to-day and long-term management of the school.

## Market analysis and research

Define the current market and your proposed offerings. Describe the demographics, trends, and market niches uncovered by your market research. You will need to show financial institutions how you conducted market research and provide them with actual proof. Explain how you will reach new customers and what strategies you will use in the future to keep customers coming to your school. You will also need to explain what resources you will require to get additional funds needed for further market research and application. (See Chapter 6 for more information on market research.)

## Technological strategy

List all the necessary technological resources you currently need, and are likely to need to successfully move on to the next stage of your business. For example, someday you will want to buy a more powerful computer or digital camera so you can upload artwork. Also consider the costs of upgrading your website (see Chapter 7 for more information).

## Forecasts and projections

This is the area in a financial business plan that most financial institutions look at closely. Describe your current financial position, supporting your statistics with indications of revenues and costs, including past, current, and projected profits. What do you foresee as most needed? Elaborate on how you will go about fulfilling these needs.

Two major categories of costing are fixed costs and variable costs. Fixed costs cover all the start-up expenses and items such as rent, salaries, insurance, and vehicle lease/loan. It also includes how much money you, the owner, will need to make a living. Variable costs include "raw material" (e.g., art supplies and staff), the costs of which will increase or decrease based on the volume of your projected business.

You will need to include a realistic revenue projection in your financial plan for both the short term (first two years) and the long term (three to five years). Explain your reasoning for the revenue projections and support them with market research data.

The business plan should also show a break-even point, which points to the minimum level of revenue you need to generate to stay afloat (i.e., enough to cover the costs before making any profits). The financial formula to figure out your break-even point is: *fixed costs* divided by *profit margin* equals *break-even point*. (The profit margin is the difference between sales and the cost of goods/services sold.)

It is possible that during the initial years you may not realistically expect to reach the break-even point, but your business plan should show when you expect it will happen and how the accumulated losses will be recovered in the later years.

If you are preparing a financial business plan for a new venture and you do not have any previous hands-on experience, you may not be aware of all the cost-related elements of your particular venture. This could result in a flawed business plan. Consulting an industry specialist, such as your accountant or lawyer, or getting the plan vetted by an accountant who has sufficient audit experience with your line of business are good ways to avoid problems.

Do not underestimate the start-up marketing costs and costs involved in running a business. You need to remember that financial institutions employ financial experts. You need to show them that you are realistic by doing your homework. It is important to establish a professional relationship with an accountant and business lawyer early on so he or she can also help with the following matters:

- Business setup
- Business registration
- Bank loan negotiations
- Yearly audits
- Tax issues (e.g., government taxes, payroll tax, or corporate tax)
- Contracts
- Liability issues

For additional help with financial business planning, contact your local small business administration office for a list of professionals in your area, or ask around.

Your bank should advise you of their specific requirements for your particular business. There are many in-depth financial business plan packages that you can get from your financial institution. Ask your bank for their own preferred business plans and requirements for small businesses they deal with as clients.

There are many resources available to small businesses. In the US you can go to the Small Business Administration (SBA) website at www.sba.gov/smallbusinessplanner/index.html for information on writing a business plan.

In Canada, you can download TD Bank's Business Planner software from www.tdcanadatrust.com/smallbusiness/planner.jsp, or go to the RBC's website at www.rbcroyalbank.com/sme/. RBC also has a planning guide at www.rbcroyalbank.com/sme/bigidea/.

As mentioned, there are detailed examples in business books (general and specific) showing exactly what business plans can look like. Research books for retail, manufacturing, or service-related businesses, and then create your own plan tailored to your own goals, staff, shareholder and venture partnerships, and financial loans (if needed).

When I set out to calculate all the business start-up costs and studied every available service-related business plan in books and on CDs, I was intent on creating the best financial strategy so that I could make my banker sit up and respect my business vision. Although I was veering toward staying in my home-based studio, which meant I would not need a business loan, I looked into the other options such as renting a studio, and which involved calculating projected expenses. If I decided to rent, I wanted to be able to convince the financial institution to lend me the funds, which would have been $20,000 to $25,000.

Sample 3 shows you how to organize your projected income and costs. For a blank spreadsheet, see the Projected Income and Operating Expenses on the CD-ROM.

To get a realistic picture of the start-up finances required you should create a spreadsheet. These one-time start-up costs can include redecoration or renovation, creation of a brand and logo, and initial website development, to name a few.

A good resource is Angie Mohr's book *Financial Management 101: Get a Grip on Your Business Numbers* (another title in the Self-Counsel Business Series). Her book is an indepth but easy-to-read guide on business planning.

I also suggest you spend some time with your accountant, who can explain and prepare you for expected and unforeseen expenses so you are better equipped to make the right financial decisions at this crucial time.

## Reality Check

Are you really ready to start up or expand your business at this time? Perhaps preparing an extensive business plan, at the very beginning or once you have spent some time with your business, is showing you areas that need to be addressed. Having thought through the ideas in more detail, you may see those areas potentially causing serious problems in the future. If you are not prepared to sacrifice as much as the start-up or expansion plan demands, then creating this plan will have served you well. It may have saved you years of energy, money, and other worries.

Your wisest option now is to take a step back and spend more time planning your business in detail. Elaborate and delve deeper into those points and potential problems that became apparent the first time you wrote your business plan, and try to close all loopholes. Establish a solid foundation. Get back on the right track to get to that next step.

## Revisiting Your Business Plan

Take stock at every opportunity to review the following details:

- Where the plan is taking you
- Where you can expand and what you can do next
- How to get to the next level

Revisit your plan regularly — visit it once a week to make sure you are on the right track and every three months with a focus on the bigger picture.

# SAMPLE 3
# PROJECTED INCOME AND OPERATING COSTS

|  | Aug | Sep | Oct | Nov | Dec |
|---|---|---|---|---|---|
| **Projected Income** | | | | | |
| Classes | 0 | 1000 | 1000 | 1000 | 1200 |
| Parties | 400 | 200 | 400 | 100 | 500 |
| After school classes | 0 | 600 | 600 | 600 | 600 |
| Seasonal camps | 3000 | 0 | 200 | 0 | 400 |
| Onsite lunch | 0 | 0 | 0 | 0 | 0 |
| Art supplies | 200 | 140 | 160 | 60 | 200 |
| Other: | | | | | |
| **Total Income** | **$3,600** | **$1,940** | **$2,360** | **$1,760** | **$2,900** |
| | | | | | |
| **Operating Costs** | | | | | |
| Accounting & legal | 50 | 50 | 50 | 50 | 50 |
| Advertising & promotion | 50 | 50 | 50 | 50 | 100 |
| Bank charges & interest | 5 | 5 | 5 | 5 | 5 |
| Fees & dues | 0 | 80 | 0 | 0 | 0 |
| Insurance | 100 | 100 | 100 | 100 | 100 |
| Materials and supplies | 200 | 100 | 100 | 100 | 150 |
| Office supplies | 25 | 0 | 0 | 0 | 25 |
| Meals & entertainment | 300 | 0 | 0 | 0 | 0 |
| Travel | 50 | 20 | 20 | 0 | 0 |
| Telephone & fax | 30 | 30 | 30 | 30 | 30 |
| Utilities | 80 | 80 | 80 | 80 | 80 |
| Staff wages & benefits | 600 | 300 | 300 | 300 | 300 |
| Website development | 300 | 0 | 0 | 0 | 0 |
| Website upgrades | 60 | 0 | 0 | 0 | 0 |
| Miscellaneous | | | | | |
| Other: | | | | | |
| **Total Costs** | **$1,850** | **$815** | **$735** | **$715** | **$840** |

You may see things differently than when you first wrote it. You may decide you can eliminate certain items (e.g., classes that are not in huge demand). You may decide you need to delegate some responsibilities as your business grows; for example, website design or maintenance, bookkeeping, or publicity. And you may realize that as you grow, increasing your publicity or certain market research tactics may prove very fruitful.

## Second draft of the business plan

As I spent more time with my plan and actually working with people, more ideas began to form. As I grew busier I began to develop a bigger vision. I learned from experience what I was doing right and what I could improve upon. I asked for honest feedback from students and staff, and I listened to what customers said they wanted and needed that was not being offered elsewhere. I saw potential in marketing and offering additional services, and growing from a few art classes a week to something more substantial. I was etching out my niche market.

Seven months after I had opened the doors for classes, I had to know if it was time to expand the business. Before I venturing into the next phase I compiled a fresh SCOT analysis. This method, which I discussed in Chapter 1, constantly helps me to make business and personal decisions. I also revisited my original action plan and goals list and asked myself the following questions:

- Do I feel ready to expand?
- Is it practical to do so?
- Where do I go next?

- How committed am I to growing this venture?
- What have I learned from my previous experiences and from my network of contacts and friends?
- What have I learned from actually doing the business in the past year that can help me improve my services and add value?

Sample 4 is an example of my SCOT analysis when I was revisiting the Jolly Good Art business plan. Based on this soul-searching and honest appraisal, I created a new, in-depth business plan, also with the help of resources such as books and websites.

See Sample 5 for my initial start-up action plan, and Sample 6 for my revised action plan that encapsulated my short- and long-term goals. Then look to Exercise 14 (on page 85), which will help you to define and clarify any vague areas in your business plan, as well as form a foundation of realistic and achievable goals that you will always have on hand.

# Bookkeeping

Here we discuss the reasons and benefits of bookkeeping, and the importance of effective record keeping.

## What is bookkeeping and why keep up-to-date records?

At the beginning there are many reasons you should do your own bookkeeping. You will get a better grasp of how your business runs and make more informed business decisions by —

## SAMPLE 4
# SCOT ANALYSIS: REVISITING THE JOLLY GOOD ART BUSINESS PLAN

| Strengths | Challenges |
|---|---|
| • Passion for art<br>• Focus/determination to succeed<br>• Spouse's moral support<br>• Clear goals<br>• Interest in learning new things<br>• Few start-up funds needed<br>• Willing to work hard<br>• Creativity/innovativeness<br>• Adaptability/flexibility | • Little time to spend with child<br>• Managing family commitments<br>• Fear of failure (sometimes)<br>• Home-based studio<br>• Lack of a long business track record |
| **Opportunities** | **Threats** |
| • Networking/contacts<br>• School contacts<br>• Neighbors and daughter's friends<br>• Expansion and big success<br>• Transferable skills from previous business<br>• Lessons learned from actual practice | • Competition<br>• Stress |

- observing the business's progress,

- determining your profitability,

- monitoring expenses (e.g., staff and materials), and

- monitoring income.

Facts and figures are fresh in your mind as you update financial records, of all that is incoming and outgoing, and what expenses are deductible. Keeping your books organized is key. It means you can locate receipts and other documents promptly. There will be no panic as tax season looms because your documents will be organized and you will be ready to hand in your tax returns with all supporting information.

At the start-up stage it is cheaper and wiser to do your own bookkeeping, to keep your finger on the ever-quickening pulse of your business. You will also save bookkeeping fees. As your business grows, you may want to eventually delegate this to a professional bookkeeper.

Scheduling a couple of hours a week for bookkeeping is a good habit that will keep documents off your desk. This helps avoid a backlog and hours of your time searching and trying to remember which items correspond with which bills. You will not have that nagging feeling about the growing mountain of paperwork.

**Mission/Goals**

To provide art classes after school and on Sundays (mornings and afternoons). In addition to offering services from my own home studio, I will travel to community centers and private schools and centers.

**Things to Do**

- Arrange for insurance
- Conduct market research about competition, pricing, and what is being offered locally. Gauge demand and what is missing in the area.
- Get friends and their children's feedback on what they liked and did not like in other art establishments as well as in my own.
- List art supplies and books needed.
- Find discounts for bulk art materials from major art supply stores and small local shops.
- Research to buy a color printer for promotional literature.
- Set up area in basement for art classes to keep start-up costs to a minimum.
- Make a list of the absolute "must haves" and "wants" and know the difference between the two. For example:

I must have the following:

- 3 tables (4 or 5 feet long)
- 12 stackable chairs
- Art supplies: variety of media, sketchpads, canvas, etc.

I want to have the following:

- Photocopier and scanner
- Faster laser printer
- Upgraded PC (with more memory)
- Digital camera (to upload students' and my own artwork)

**Research**

- Promotion
- General awareness of my services
- Mutual referrals
- Bulk discount deals from galleries, framers, and other creative and recreational establishments.

**Staff**

To work on my own for the first year with assistants as needed.

**Target Market**

Students who want to learn how to draw, paint with watercolors, oils, acrylics, and gouache, paint on glass, and make collages.

**Demographics**

Gauge for potential receptiveness to distribution of leaflets. Give leaflets and other promotional materials to students, all residents within a five- to six-mile radius of studio, as well as to libraries and art supply stores.

**Competition**

- A small art school with an attached gallery and summer art camp within a four-mile radius of my place of business.
- An art teacher who arranges art-and-craft activities for birthday parties for large groups of young children.

The competitors' advantages include —

- Taking more children at a time (i.e., from 15 to 25 students)
- Having an established name
- Being located near a shopping mall and not in a residential area
- A large client base

My advantages include —

- Art and creative discovery along with fun in much smaller groups with emphasis on individual attention.
- Running a business that is not commercialized.

---

If you are unfamiliar with bookkeeping, read books on the topic and check out hands-on user-friendly accounting software such as QuickBooks. In today's world of advanced computer technology, record keeping can be extremely easy. Choose the financial accounting and record-keeping system that will encourage you to keep documents up to date and regularly filed. This will help you monitor your income and expenses. It will also help you be prepared for tax season.

When looking for accounting software, find one you can easily customize for your particular business needs. Ensure that it encourages regular use and is flexible should your current and future plans change. Use a trial system for a full three weeks to really see if it is effective for you. If you are having trouble deciding on a program, ask a bookkeeping contact. Accounting software introduces more structure to the day-to-day running of a business.

Another good resource is Angie Mohr's Numbers 101 for Small Business series. In particular, her book *Bookkeepers' Boot Camp: Get a Grip on Accounting Basics* will help you

# START-UP ACTION PLAN B

**Mission Statement**

Jolly Good Art Studio provides creative art classes and services to stimulate and develop artists' self-expression and talents in a nurturing and fun environment.

**Things to Do**

- Register Jolly Good Art name and business
- Secure domain name and hosting package for website
- Secure large studio with own entrance and large outdoor area for summer activities
- Review liability insurance (i.e., check full coverage for increased student traffic)
- Take refresher First-Aid and Coronary and Pulmonary Resuscitation (CPR) courses (all staff)
- Increase services as demand rises for various camps, birthday parties, charity craft weekends, and adult classes

**Staff**

- Interview and hire more staff
- Add more specialized staff to accommodate larger groups of students for seasonal camps

**Classes**

- Develop new programs that would benefit and excite new and current students. Ask students and their parents for their suggestions about how to continually improve the business's quality of service and customer satisfaction.
- Expand creative programs (e.g., silk painting, clay modeling, and mosaics)

**Website**

- Get hosting package
- Design and maintain for information and awareness
- Use for promotion of services
- Use for free press and advertising
- Write and post articles
- Create contests and draws
- Showcase students' work
- Create a calendar featuring students' artwork
- Advertise annual or biannual art exhibitions for self-esteem and brand awareness, both on website and in studio

**Long-Term Objectives**

- Organize retreats
- Organize weekend outings
- Sell art supplies
- Research partnership or collaborations

# EXERCISE 14
# VISUALIZE YOUR ACTION PLAN

1. What is the true focus of your business services? (Write down your mission statement.)

2. What is your strategic direction and vision? (Describe it in detail.)

3. What do you need to get started?

4. How long will it take before you can start?

5. How do you plan to get there?

6. Where do you plan to go next?

7. Complete a SCOT analysis of your plan. (Write down the challenges you want to work toward eliminating and the opportunities you envision based on your market research. The threats may include competition or financial constraints, but consider how these threats can be turned into positive factors.)

8. If you are already offering services to clients and are considering expanding, which direction do your strongest opportunities point you toward?

to learn the basics of your income and cash flow statement as well as how to account for your inventory. She also includes some good tips on how to manage paper flow to keep organized.

When you are ready to expand and delegate your bookkeeping, you will have a grounded knowledge of what is involved in bookkeeping and you will be able to give the bookkeeper professionally organized books to take over the process. This will make your life, as well as the bookkeeper's, easier.

## Bookkeeping: How simple or how complicated?

For the first six months to a year of my own enterprise, I opted to do my own bookkeeping for the reasons I just mentioned — to save professional fees as well as to feel the pulse of my business's progress. I started off with a very basic hard copy system that may seem archaic to most people in this technologically advanced era! If you would like to do it the way I did, the bookkeeping templates and notebooks available for small- and medium-sized businesses are more than adequate.

I used two triplicate books to log all sales and transaction records: a black notebook to record incoming sales, which was the money received and revenue generated; and a red book to record accounts payable, which was the outgoing expenses and bills paid.

I kept customer receipts in a blue triplicate book, with all the customers' details for future reference, and all the receipts for art supplies and other such expenses in a separate, appropriately named file.

As I expanded the business, Excel spreadsheets and QuickBooks software came into play for quicker bookkeeping and record keeping.

## Personal cash flow chart

I also became much more serious about charting and monitoring my personal cash flow activities, such as housekeeping and family expenses. All of this counts and has a direct impact on the business. For example, you and your accountant can calculate the percentage of your personal and household expenses (e.g., phone, heating and electricity bills, gas, vehicle insurance, and mortgage or rent payments), which you can claim against your business taxes. Be very precise with your calculations on your personal cash flow chart.

To monitor your cash flow activities, use Form 6.

## FORM 6
# PERSONAL CASH FLOW STATEMENT

| Income | Monthly |
|---|---|
| My salary | |
| Spouse's salary | |
| Investment income | |
| Personal art sales | |
| Other: | |

| Fixed Expenses | Monthly |
|---|---|
| Family needs | |
| Food | |
| Clothing | |
| Personal grooming | |
| Mortgage/rent | |
| Car payment | |
| Car insurance | |
| Car maintenance and repairs | |
| Gasoline | |
| License and registration | |
| Home insurance | |
| Home repairs | |
| Property taxes | |
| Home telephone | |
| Cell phone | |
| Gas and electricity | |
| Water bill | |
| Credit card | |
| Loans | |
| Other: | |

| Other Expenses | Monthly |
|---|---|
| Vacations | |
| Entertainment | |
| Charitable donations | |
| Gifts | |
| Other: | |

| Savings | Monthly |
|---|---|
| Investments | |
| Other: | |

# 6

# IDENTIFYING AND TARGETING YOUR MARKET

*I keep six honest serving-men*
*(They taught me all I knew);*
*Their names are What and Why and When*
*And How and Where and Who.*

— RUDYARD KIPLING

This chapter covers the magnitude and range of market research, advertising, and promotion. This chapter will help you make informed choices when it comes to your clients and your competition.

## What Is Marketing?

There are many theories about marketing. The most effective marketing involves getting across the message that a business is focused on customers and the satisfaction of their needs. The "marketing concept" means satisfying your customer needs and should be at the heart of every business decision you make. Without happy return customers you will have no business.

Copywriter Patricia Ruhl says, "Marketing is about identifying your customers' needs and then fulfilling them, profitably." A plethora of activities fall under the marketing umbrella, including market research, sales, sales promotion, public relations, and advertising. These are critical components of your marketing machine. As you start your marketing engine, consider the four major types of gas that gets things moving: price, place, product, and promotion — otherwise known as the "marketing mix" (more on this later). Used in combination to a greater or lesser degree, these components fuel the success of your marketing efforts.

The purpose of market research is to help you identify the effectiveness and feasibility of your advertising and your services. You formulate strategies by analyzing supply and demand. How much are your school's services needed?

The following are times when you will need to conduct and implement market research:

- Before starting your business
- When you are mining/prospecting for new clients and recommendations
- When you are deciding whether or not to offer new services or diversify to keep your clientele healthy, growing, and thriving
- And in fact, all the time, so you can constantly improve your services

## Direct and indirect marketing

Direct marketing means promoting your services directly to your targeted audience. To get a customer's attention you may distribute leaflets, flyers, and emails. You may want to contact the following people with your direct advertising:

- Current, prospective, and referred clients
- Those who have inquired previously
- Teachers and previous contacts
- Those you network with, professionally and socially

Indirect marketing uses a more subtle approach by getting your name out there in public without making it look like you are trying to get business. The following are some indirect marketing strategies I used:

- Giving donations at charity auctions

- Holding raffles that gave away a free lesson, course, or camp day, or a discount voucher
- Organizing students' exhibitions
- Fund-raising and doing arts and crafts for charity events (in my studio or on a larger scale)
- Volunteering and teaching free art lessons at schools, libraries, and community centers
- Writing articles and lesson plans for specialist magazines and newspapers
- Encouraging students and their parents to invite their friends and relatives to join classes

## The Marketing Mix

The "marketing mix" is a marketing term coined by Neil H. Borden and includes the four Ps: price, place, product, and promotion. I have added to this — people, promotion, and practice — and compiled my own list of Ps, derived from my successful marketing planning and experiences:

- *Place*: Location of your target audience
- *People*: Customers, competition, and networking
- *Promotion*: Advertising, brand awareness, and reputation
- *Process*: Getting from concept to end result for the customer (discussed in Chapter 1)
- *Product*: Unique and compelling services and packages (discussed in Chapter 3)

- *Price*: Value, competitive pricing, and incentives (discussed in Chapter 4)

- *Practice*: Delivering the best all-around experience

I will focus on the first three Ps in this chapter: place, people, and promotion. The rest of the Ps have been discussed in more detail in previous chapters, but you will see how all the Ps tie together once you have an understanding of what marketing means to your business.

You can mix the above Ps as you would mix ingredients for a cake. The recipe changes depending on the situation, the customer, and the customer's needs. When you are trying to increase enrolment for an exciting new program or product, you might need a little more sugar — that is, *price incentive*. You might want to add other ingredients such as *promoting at the local community center*, as well as *distributing your studio's flyers*. Rejig the mix accordingly as you strive to fill your customers' needs and you have experienced the power of marketing.

If you miss out on any of the seven Ps, the imbalance can ruin your whole marketing strategy. Remember, your school's success is a direct result of your customers' satisfaction. When they are satisfied they will recommend your programs to others and your business will grow.

Be proactive about identifying and exceeding your clients' wants, needs, and expectations, in the short term as well as the long term. You are aiming to constantly "over-deliver," that is, to create and offer the right service, in the right place, to the right audience, at the right time, and at the right price.

# Place: Location of Your Target Audience

The first thing you need to do is find your target market. In the beginning, I concentrated on the local area, within a five-mile radius of my initial location. This was my local community. The community as a whole became my research ground. I learned from everyone and anyone that spoke to me about the demand and supply for my new venture.

There are many ways to carry out market research. Primary research is the information that is all around us — research carried out directly ourselves — and includes what we already know. Talking to people, observing social and financial behavior, and conducting surveys can provide you with primary research.

Secondary research can be found going on the Internet, reading books and published studies, and watching TV programs. Secondary research also includes demographic information, which is all about facts and figures. Go to the US Census Bureau's website at http://quickfacts.census.gov, or if you are in Canada, to Statistics Canada's website at www.statcan.ca. You can also find demographic information in printed publications at the library, although it may not be as up to date as what you will find online.

To understand the attitudes, values, and fears of your target audience, researching *psychographics* will help you understand and identify the "how" and "why" of your targeted clients' decisions. The best way I have found this information is by using my primary research skills and talking and asking

# RESEARCH IN THE CONCEPTION STAGES

| Ideal Customers | Demographics | Psychographics |
|---|---|---|
| Child: teens and younger children | 5 to 18 years of age | • Artistic<br>• Creative<br>• Resourceful<br>• Needing a challenge<br>• Returning to art<br>• Open to new things<br>• Looking to develop themselves creatively<br>• Vary according to level of comprehension and communication skills |
| Adult: parents, young and middle-aged adults, seniors | 18 years of age and older, including moms and dads, retirees, married, divorced, single | |
| Special needs | 5 years of age and older | |
| Community as a whole | Healthcare professionals who deal with children with special needs | |
| Schools | Students | |
| Community groups | Community center programs such as dance, yoga, and pottery. | |

questions to the right people (i.e., parents, children, and teachers). Encourage honest comments and suggestions, knowing that some people may feel uncomfortable in giving personal opinions that may not be fully complimentary or positive. When you encourage and receive frank suggestions and ideas from your customers, it will improve the school's services, and everybody wins.

Sample 7 is an example of how I went about discovering my ideal customers by using demographics and psychographics.

The market research you conduct before you start will show you the demand and the type of services students require and what is available in your locality. Talk to your local real estate agent. Real estate agents are full of invaluable information about your local community. Your relationship with realtors may eventually result in them recommending your services and vice versa.

When your school is up and running, you can continue your market research by getting your students' input. Create student surveys to get specific information and ideas to implement in your classes and your summer camps. This feedback can be quite valuable. (See Form 4, the Seasonal Camp Survey, in Chapter 3.)

With the help of your answers to Exercise 15 you will start to get a clear vision of who your real target market is.

# People: Customers, Competition, and Networking

Your customers, competition, and networking contacts will all come into play when

## EXERCISE 15
## TARGETING YOUR MARKET

Use creative visualization to envision your potential clients/students.

1.  What are the backgrounds of your target clients/students?



2.  What types of occupations do the students or their parents have (e.g., still at school, business owners, employees, retirees, stay-at-home parents, or caregivers)?



3.  What is the income range for your students or their parents?



4.  What is the marital status of your students or their parents?



5.  What are the hobbies and interests of your students or their parents?



6.  What special benefits will your services provide to these clients/students?

marketing your business. Stay realistic about your daily schedule, regulate your marketing activities, and do not aim blindly, hoping to reach a mass audience. Instead, start by targeting a small select group. Over time and with perseverance, your client base will increase and inevitably become much more aware of your unique brand and services.

## Customers

I found that whenever I became too engrossed in the other aspects of the business and did not make an extra effort to call and communicate with clients (which included sending them reminders and telling them about incentives), the phrase "out of sight, out of mind" became true. I had to make sure I kept in touch in some way, and that people stayed in touch with Jolly Good Art. I have always maintained that if I get any suggestions and ideas that may improve the school's services, everybody wins.

When asking your customers for feedback, remember that you cannot please everyone 100 percent of the time. And there may be comments or points of view that you do not agree with. Thank your customers for sharing their time and effort in answering your questions. Write down any recommendations they have and think about what they said. Customers see things from a different perspective. Try and walk in their shoes, and get insight into how they see things. Discover ways to come to long-term win-win collaborations.

Listen to your customers. And listen to people you are marketing to who are not interested in your services. Although I prefer the "straight up" approach, many people opt to be polite or noncommittal. I have learned there are many different ways to say no, and

that many people don't want to get into such a conversation, feeling uncomfortable about giving any feedback. Although it may help the school, they would rather not get involved. Some customers may even be afraid they may be coerced into committing to something they do not want. I always made it clear that all I wanted from them was information so that I could improve the school's services and students' experiences.

If the customer refuses to answer your questions, do not take it personally. Or if you do receive honest criticism, learn from it and move on.

Mine fresh territory for new clients continually. There is an abundance of prospective artists to whom you can become a teacher. Who is your ideal customer? Keep your list of prospects as wide as possible. As an entrepreneur you should see everyone you meet and every situation as an opportunity for gathering more clients. The following list includes where and to whom you can market:

- Your friends

- Your children's friends

- Your community (e.g., churches, recreational centers, cultural centers, daycare centers)

- Public and private schools

- Grocery stores

- Coffee shops

- Places that offer extracurricular activities (e.g., yoga, dance, pottery)

- Doctors and pediatricians

- Caregivers of children with special needs

- Counselors and therapists (for families and children)

You have to communicate with parents as well as the students themselves to find out what they want and expect. Listen closely. As discussed earlier, know the demographics, including the age ranges and the number of families, in your targeted area.

You will find that your target audience may change with time (along with your marketing strategies). It may become much more specific. You may even specialize in certain media that become popular with your clients. Perhaps you will decide to hone in on the children's market. You may find that marketing to busy parents who prioritize their family's and others' needs before their own results in low attendance rates.

The retired or semiretired population may be a reliable and even lucrative source of income. You may also find it more rewarding, both emotionally and professionally. You are at service to a community and you get to see talent being born or rediscovered.

Exercise 16 will help you discover your customers' needs.

# Competition

A few of my older students came to Jolly Good Art from a large art school in the area. There was an obvious deficiency in the competition's services — my students expressed that they felt like they were treated like a number rather than as an individual artist. What they found refreshing at Jolly Good Art was all the steps the teachers and I took to learn exactly what their individual needs and aspirations were.

No two artists or schools are the same, and there are many ways they can be compatible. You must make sure yours is the perfect fit to attract and keep as many happy clients as possible. Disappointed customers will vote with their feet. Just as they may have come to you from a competing school seeking a better quality of service, they will leave your school if you do not deliver what they need.

Consider your competition. Where are they located? What makes your business different from theirs? Are you and are they keeping up with the trends? Do not be threatened by what you perceive to be the success of your competitors. We all have to figure out our missing links by observing our competition. From a student's point of view, study the competition's website, programs, and actual delivery. What are they missing that you know is important to the customers?

Believe in yourself. You have original and fresh ideas that will come out alive against the competition.

In my opinion there is also such a thing as doing too much preparation work. Do not "over-research" and let the competition paralyze you or dissuade you from your path and vision.

Whenever people believe there is little or no competition to worry about, they are living in hope and/or they have not done proper research. If there are really no services such as yours in your area, you are either living in a very remote area where art teaching services aren't needed, or you are in a new suburban area in which people are getting only some of their artistic needs met

## EXERCISE 16
# KNOW YOUR CLIENTS

1.  What are the demographics of your target market (i.e., age and family composition)?

2.  What are your potential client's perceived and real needs and wants?

3.  How can you reach your target market (e.g., through brand awareness, website promotions, showcasing students' art, discounts, door-to-door flyers, etc.)?

4.  Is there an established market for your services in your area?

5.  Where do your friends' children and your children's friends and classmates go for art or similar recreational activities?

6.  Is your studio in a neighborhood that includes many families or a significant number of seniors?

7.  Is it in a residential area near schools or other community-oriented services?

at school, at church, or at home. In the latter case, you are in the position to pioneer an art teaching business in this area.

If you have gauged enough initial interest from prospective customers, this is a perfect opportunity you must seize. Chances are, you will find yourself in a community with welcoming neighbors, in which your services will become a popular commodity. Popularity will motivate you to keep up with the growing demand and provide even better service.

If you are the pioneering school or establishment in the area, you should do the following:

- Prepare and plan for rapid growth to keep up with demand.

- Make sure you are reasonably and realistically priced to cover your costs but not overpriced because of an apparent monopoly.

- Prepare to meet a spectrum of needs for a spectrum of customers.

- Strategize for the possibility that competing services will crop up around you. After all, you are proof there is a lucrative market for this service.

Rest assured, just as you have approached people, whether to check out your competition (in this example you would have gone outside of your own area) or to interview prospective students in your community, people will approach you too. They may have never taken their children to art lessons, but are willing to take them to you as "artistic guinea pigs."

If you live in a larger community, accept the fact that there is a healthy amount of competition around you. Do not be overwhelmed or discouraged. See this as yet another opportunity for growth and advancement. Let it push you harder, and enjoy the challenge of taking charge and staying ahead of your competition.

Anticipate change. Your business and the market are ever-evolving. You have to be flexible with the wind of progress and with the unexpected. If you shove your head in the sand, someone will come along — it could even be one of your former employees — and open up an even better school with all the bells and whistles you were too busy to plan ahead for or to think of. Prevent and prepare for such contingencies by frequently reviewing your business plan, marketing strategies, and long-term goals.

By keeping your finger on the pulse of trends and being aware of the importance of constant growth, you will stand out and become a great creative and educational powerhouse, which your customers — as well as your employees — will be proud to be a part of.

Exercise 17 will help you discover who your competition is and what you should do differently from them, including building your own unique marketing strategy. Keep up to date so you can better supply what clients need and want, and then promote and make people aware of your unique services.

## Networking

Networking is an important skill you have to develop over time. Keep track of who you

## EXERCISE 17
## YOUR COMPETITORS

1. Who is your competition?


2. How are your particular teaching style and programs different from those already offered? (This is where you need to focus on your artistic and creative strengths.)


3. What are you better at or what do you offer that your competitors do not provide? (At Jolly Good Art it was the small groups — each student always had individual attention — and the teachers' creative approach.)


4. What are the current trends? What are students' current likes and dislikes — in and outside art — whether it is their choice of electronic gizmos, games, movies, or TV programs? What else do they do for entertainment?


5. What type of advertising techniques do your competitors use?


6. Do you think your competitors' advertisements are effective? Why or why not?

know, and create mutually beneficial relationships. (Of course be careful that you are not taking advantage of anyone.) As this is an integral part of business, Chapter 9 is dedicated to this topic. Consider your networking contacts, in and outside your business circle, as research subjects or as prospective clients or people who would know prospective clients.

Communicate with local schoolteachers, parents, friends, neighbors, people who work at community centers, and day-care providers. What is consistently missing in the curricula? What is in demand? Keep their future goals in mind, as you may find an initiative you can incorporate later into your programs.

Politicians at all levels can also be good to form an alliance with. Talk to the local town authorities and build a rapport with them. You never know how you will be able to help them and how they can help you. Check out local corporations as well. Do they focus on a specific sector when it comes to charitable donations? How can you be part of that?

Be proactive. Donate an art class through charity auctions. Not only are you networking, you are building awareness of your business in the community.

Networking is a science and an art that brings dividends at various stages. My relationship with local school principals led me to seek permission from regional school boards to advertise my services to their students. Because I was aware of what the school authorities were striving to achieve, I realized that my services would mesh perfectly with their vision.

Networking never ends, and additional connections never hurt. See how you can collaborate together; perhaps you could share advertising space and costs, or organize a special joint-effort event in aid of charity or the community.

## Promotion: Advertising, Brand Awareness, and Reputation

Now that you have figured out who your target market is, developed your services, and discovered your short- and long-term visions, you need to bring attention to your services. You know exactly what you are offering and are always fine-tuning what you offer, but if not enough people know about you in the first place, the success will take much longer than you may have projected in your business plan. Of course you should try bringing attention to your school and its services in a way that is the least costly and has the maximum effect.

There are many ways to reach your prospective clients. The following list will give you some ideas:

- Distributing leaflets at doctors' offices, community centers, libraries, schools, and framing stores

- Creating incentives for current clients to recommend new clients

- Advertising in newspapers, trade magazines, specialist publications that feature local or state/provincial program calendars, parenting magazines, and the Yellow Pages

- Advertising online in children-oriented resource directories (in Vancouver and Toronto, check out www.helpwevegotkids.com, and in Ontario, check out www.ourkidsareworthit.com)

- Advertising on bulletin boards in schools, churches, and art or craft supply stores

- Organizing raffle draws or donating a free class or course at charity auctions

- Holding art classes and demonstrations at local community centers, schools, libraries, and art or craft supply stores

- Designing a great website and offering incentives online

## Advertising

As a well-rounded businessperson you will learn to specialize in all aspects of direct marketing: sales, advertising, public relations, and promotion. The secret is to do as much as possible, on the cheapest budget, with the highest quality and most return of effectiveness.

Keep a close eye on your advertising budget and consider whether it is being spent in the best possible way. Review other options such as giving incentives for current clients to recommend your school's services. Is there any way that you can advertise for free, or get free press?

Balance your promotion and advertising tactics with creating new and innovative programs that would naturally bring more attention to your school. And speak to everyone — clients, the press, as well as your network of contacts. Keep track of how effective your promotional efforts are by asking your clients directly or through surveys.

Marketing, publicity, and advertising will eat away the biggest part of the budget. Large companies persistently inject vast amounts of money into all this because it works for them. As long as they keep pushing their product in a constant, steady manner they become a recognized and trusted brand.

A home-based art teaching business can successfully promote itself using four basic strategies:

- Word-of-mouth recommendations

- Having a good network of people in the community and the press

- Offering discounts and free trial classes

- Dynamic web presence

From my experience, between 5 percent and 10 percent of all paid advertising is successful, and only if you advertise regularly. Until you have more insight and experience with how and where your money is most effectively used, avoid experimenting with costlier methods by trial and error.

As you plan your advertising strategies, do the following:

- Consult those in your network who can share their experiences with you, and ask them what traits and strengths they see about your business that you can highlight in your promotion and advertising campaigns

- Contact market research experts (they are available for a fee)

- Learn from the competition and from similar schools worldwide, studying what you like and do not like about other schools' techniques — what appears to work and what you would do differently

### Word-of-mouth advertising

Whether you are starting out or getting established, the best way to get business is through word-of-mouth referrals. It is free advertising, basically. People trust their friends' recommendations more than a published advertisement.

Although it is a universally known fact that you cannot please everyone all the time, you should aim for the "highly pleased" mark 99.9 percent of the time. You are obligated to the children and their parents to make the experience of learning art enjoyable and fun, whether it is in class, at a birthday party, or at a seasonal camp. And this has a domino effect, increasing your studio's client base. As you earn more trust, your school's success will grow as well.

### Writing articles

Another form of free advertising is writing and publishing articles. Your expertise in art, hobbies, parenthood, etc. will become evident and your name will be increasingly on people's minds.

If you've never written an article before, why not try now? All you do is become your own interviewer. We are all storytellers — now make it work for you. Many people enjoy hearing about other people's interesting quirks and the stories behind their successes. What kind of questions would you ask if you interviewed someone like yourself who had a similar business and artistic background? You can even think about writing a simple blog (short for "web log," i.e., a computerized journal) on your website.

You should at least learn how to write a media release, or get professional help with it. The gist of a media release is to cover the "who, what, why, where, and when" of something related to your business that you believe may be of interest to the press and to the community.

As you research where you could publish articles, study the following types of publications and think about the interesting and quirky ways you, as a writer, can distinguish yourself:

- Newspapers (local and national)
- School newsletters
- Trade magazines, trade books, and websites related to the following:
    - art
    - health
    - parenting
    - teaching
    - business
    - caregiving of those with special needs
    - psychology
    - self-improvement

All of this reading will serve you on many levels, teaching you about trends, changes, and educational needs. It is, of course, much more than just finding out the submission requirements so you can contribute articles to them. With the information you glean from these sources, by immersing yourself in and keeping abreast of media, you will be able to confidently approach them with what you have to offer.

I keep all the newspaper and magazine cuttings that catch my eye, even website printouts and advertisements, in a large "To Be Read" folder and keep it handy near where I have my breaks. I read an article or two and then move them to another file for later review, or as a reminder. Even if I never read the profile, advertisement, website, or article again, I will remember the gist of it if I see it in the file. These are ready for my brainstorming sessions, or if there is a dilemma or an angle I have to work through.

If, for example, I am about to be interviewed or I am writing an article or a business profile for a newspaper, I will look over the media clippings for inspiration. In my experience anything that deals with family values, success in one's personal life or business, and genuine and sincere passion for any human endeavor (this can be a recreational activity or anything that involves self-improvement), are always appreciated by readers. The more you soak up about your environment and its people, the more you will be equipped to talk about their specific needs and desires.

Approach the many parenting and family-oriented magazines, especially those that touch on psychological or artistic subjects, in order to reach out to readers who would include children, adults, parents, grandparents, other teachers, and caregivers. Those with special needs and their parents and caregivers may also like to hear your stories. Write about your art lessons, and also about general strategies that they can use to improve or change their lives in some way.

Read newspapers and keep current. Learn about the various niches, people who would make up your reading audience — for example, stay-at-home parents, caregivers, students, and businesspeople.

With experience you will gain more confidence and find more subjects to write about. What you want is to maximize exposure and reach as wide an audience as possible. People within your own community — your students, neighbors, and friends — will be proud of how well known you've become.

Expressing your personal and professional values and opinions will have a positive rippling effect and increase your credibility. And it will keep you on the community's mind as much as possible.

Complete Exercise 18 to find your target audience through your writing.

### Contact the press

If you do not want to write, or do not think you are able to write for whatever reason, consider being interviewed by the local press, especially when you have organized particular activities that would interest the community such as a charity fund-raiser or annual art exhibition of your students' artwork.

Some businesses start by allocating a specific amount of their budget to print advertising, but I find that a well-chosen interview spot in a local newspaper or on TV has much more impact.

# EXERCISE 18
# RESEARCHING AND WRITING ARTICLES

1. Which magazines, including those found online, do you read? Study old and new issues of your favorite magazines that relate to business, art, or creativity. List the magazines to which you would like to submit articles.

2. Based on the articles and the advertisements in various magazines, who are their target readers?

3. Are there other magazines that are read by a wider cross-section of your target audience?

4. What topics can you write about that would appeal to the readers of selected magazines?

5. Research the submission guidelines for various magazines and prepare query letters to editors. Do you have samples of previously published articles to submit? If not, write a short article for a targeted reader.

If you find yourself regularly interviewed by well-respected local or national journalists in trade and family magazines and newspapers, these recommendations and positive write-ups will prove to be much more effective than spending hundreds and thousands of dollars on advertisements.

You do not always have to be doing something amazing and newsworthy to attract the press or media. It is all about providing a fresh angle, especially when it comes to confirming and reaffirming the values of the community. Getting a reputation as a Samaritan by volunteering or contributing to charitable causes is very satisfying, but be sincere. Do it because you genuinely care about the causes. That said, getting a public figure you respect involved in your charitable events will likely give you more attention and exposure!

In interviews, talk about the hidden payoffs of teaching. You will no doubt have some gratifying experiences you can bring up. Perhaps an adult student's self-discovery of latent talent has led to an art-related career. Or a parent who sought to encourage his child's self-expression was inspired to take classes himself.

Free publicity will pump up and strengthen all your public relations endeavors. You can never get too much positive light shed on you and your school. Someone else's write-up is much more powerful than anything you would say. Get others to sing your praises whenever possible.

Build a rapport with the journalists you meet whose work you particularly admire, and whose opinions or style resonate with your own. Ask them out for coffee or lunch.

Remember, journalists are always looking for interesting subjects and unique angles they can explore and share with readers. Before you meet, think of all the distinctive features of your business, and why they are noteworthy.

Follow up by phone or by email with those you sent a media release package to, or those you approached personally. And do not waste your own or their time if you do not intend to take it to the next level. Schedule five of these calls or emails a week, and mark the follow-up calls in your calendar. If you send them a media release, make contact within a week or two to give them enough time to go through your information. If you are trying to promote an event or a course, this means you have to prepare your material a month or so ahead.

I had revisited my mission statement to prepare for an interview with a well-respected journalist at a local monthly magazine (with a circulation of more than 250,000 households). I was determined to convey exactly what Jolly Good Art was all about, which was —

- reaching as many creative minds as possible,

- helping people of all ages to discover and express their hidden talents,

- helping them learn artistic self-discovery and self-expression in a fun, inspiring, and safe environment, and

- enhancing and making a difference in people's lives.

I also pointed out what made my school fresh and different:

- Jolly Good Art provided a missing link in the educational curriculum.

- It was committed to enhancing the neighborhood.

- It was passionate about and paid extra attention to its programs and to serving the community.

The interview went well and the article did advertise all the points I highlighted above. After it was published I became a local celebrity! New customers came to the school saying they had read the interview and were inspired to try out Jolly Good Art.

### Share advertising costs

Advertise for less by sharing the limelight. Link to other businesses on your website, or combine your advertising campaign with that of another business. Share a page in a newspaper or produce a leaflet together.

Make sure you and the business you partner with have services that are compatible and enhance each other. For example, you could join forces with companies that offer swimming classes or yoga classes, or with a dance school, karate school, cooking school, catering service, or bakery. However, you may find that partnering up with another art school may not be feasible. You may see each other as direct competition, so such a collaboration would not work for either of you.

### Fund-raising and charitable events

There is a great feeling of accomplishment when you contribute to society and the community, especially by working for charitable organizations that mean a lot to you.

Volunteer as much time as you can spare at your local church, school, shelters, or other organizations. Not only will you be closely aware of what is happening in your community, you and your school will be considered an integral part of it. You will be a respected and valued member of society.

Jolly Good Art has initiated many fund-raising activities and made contributions to organizations such as the World Wildlife Fund (WWF), the Childhood Cancer Society, and the Autism Society. All these mean a great deal to me and my family.

A senior fund-raising organizer at the World Wildlife Fund once phoned and asked me if Jolly Good Art students would be interested in contributing artwork for the CN Tower Climb for WWF Canada. I jumped at the opportunity: The artwork, along with messages created by the students, was showcased all the way up to the top of CN Tower. This served as an energizing boost to the participants climbing the 1,776 steps of the tower — and also brought publicity to Jolly Good Art. The WWF gave the school an appreciation award, which I framed and hung with other Jolly Good Art recognition awards.

Explore causes that you and your family care about. Try and make a difference in your community and it will make a difference to your business and your life.

### Raffles

Create raffle tickets for parents and children to give them a chance to win free classes, including seasonal camps. You can set up these ballot boxes at charity events, as well as any place where you are distributing your leaflets. I would always go through the ballots, which included names, ages, addresses, and phone numbers. Children that were not old enough to take part in the classes would sometimes fill out ballots too, and I filed the information for future reference, as these children would grow up and become potential clients. I considered all the entrants as potential clients, and I called each one to gauge their interest in art. This really encouraged some of them to become clients.

You may come across a few people who are merely trying their luck to win a free gift, but you will also find people who are genuinely interested in hearing more about your services.

One idea for raffles is to offer a very tantalizing art kit as one of the prizes. Include a picture of it with the ballot box, along with several of your tri-fold leaflets. This shouldn't take up much counter space; use a colorful six-by-six inch box with a slot in the top for collecting raffle tickets.

### Trade shows

Another good strategy is to rent a booth at a trade show. This is a good way to promote your programs and get more exposure for your art school, as well as to connect not only with prospective clients, but with people who you may collaborate with in the future.

Trade shows do vary. The following are some that may work for your business:

- Career fairs
- Summer camp trade shows

- Arts and crafts trade shows (such as the "One of a Kind" shows in Toronto and Chicago)
- Franchise trade shows

Make sure your booth is as enticing as possible for passersby. The more people who stop and talk to you and your staff, the greater the chance you have of getting new clients. Decorate your booth with students' artwork as well as your own. (Remember to get permission from your students and from the parents of students younger than 18.)

Bring lots of leaflets, brochures, and business cards to hand out, and be friendly and enthusiastic about discussing your programs.

Research trade shows and find the best fit for your business and target market. Attend some of them. You may get even more ideas and inspiration for your own business. If you end up attracting great students and great staff, it may be because of all the time you spent preparing and researching!

### Leaflets

You could design leaflets (with or without a logo at first) simply using Word, PowerPoint, CorelDRAW, or any other program you may have. Print or photocopy as many as you can afford (I started with 150 in my first batch), and distribute them in as many places as you can think of. Here are some possible locations:

- Libraries
- Doctor's offices and medical clinics (pediatricians as well as family doctors)
- Dentist's offices

- Pharmacies

- Dry cleaners

- Bakeries

- Companies that offer yoga, swimming, or karate classes

- Dance studios

- Local community centers

- Framing stores. Perhaps you already have a relationship with a local framing store, having had your own artwork framed. Send your students to them too. Perhaps you can get a small discount for bulk orders. They probably won't mind displaying your school's leaflets as long as they understand you are helping each other.

- Ice-cream parlors. I had a good rapport with an owner of an ice-cream parlor who offered customized ice-cream cakes no matter what the season. I referred my students and birthday clients to her.

Another area to look into is local public and private schools. You will need to get permission from school authorities to advertise on the schools' message boards. Perhaps you can get a teacher to distribute leaflets in class.

I concentrated on a few local public schools. I successfully received permission from these schools to distribute Jolly Good Art flyers. I had called the school authorities to gauge their interest, and then I sent them a copy of my leaflet and a letter formally requesting their permission, which also included information about my school. (See Sample 8.)

## Business cards

Business cards are an important part of your business. A simply designed business card has your name, logo, and contact information. Note that it may help you get more clients: By passing it out to your family members, friends, and other people in your network, they may pass it on to others who are looking for your service.

Make sure your business card looks professional. Keep it simple. A cluttered business card with too much information will dissuade people from holding on to your card or passing it on to others. If it has a fun design and a great logo, people are more likely to keep it in their wallets and purses.

If you have a home business, you may want to include only your business phone number, website address, and email address, and avoid printing your home address. Privacy shouldn't be an issue if you have a business address outside of your home.

Even though it is a little more expensive, get your business card professionally printed on good quality paper. Do not be tempted to use business card paper from an office supply store and print cards from your own computer. People will see the difference in quality!

## Brand awareness

Brand awareness is all about name recognition. You are synonymous with your name and your logo, whether you are in a small town or large city. And just like if you were to reinvent yourself, you are creating features and characteristics to be "brand" new.

# LETTER SEEKING PERMISSION TO DISTRIBUTE
# ART LEAFLETS IN SCHOOLS

To: Regional District School Board
Attn: Ms. Smith
Date: September 1, 20--
Re: Permission to Distribute Art Leaflets

Dear Ms. Smith,

Thank you for taking the time this morning to talk to me on the phone. I have attached a copy of my Jolly Good Art leaflet that I would like to distribute to the schools in the surrounding area. The Regional District School Board has given me permission for the past few years to distribute them throughout their schools. I would like to extend my services to other schools that may also benefit from Jolly Good Art Studio's services.

With school cutbacks, art and other extracurricular activities are the first activities to be cut. It has become evident that parents are committed to finding safe environments in which their children can participate in creative projects. I am proud to say that I have a wonderful reputation as someone who is caring and inspirational to those who come to learn with me. I believe that my programs enhance the lives of my art students, build their self-esteem, and are of great benefit to all concerned.

I also urge you to look up the events section of my website, www.jollygoodartstudio.com, where you will see a news article about my daughter's "Crafts for Charities" event that prompted the principal of her school to recommend that I speak to you.

You will see that over the past few years I have been teaching art to adults, children, and children with special needs. Please review the testimonial section of my website, where many students affirm their commitment to the programs I offer.

To show my commitment to and appreciation of schools in your area, I would like to offer two to four hours per month of my art services on a voluntary basis.

I look forward to receiving your feedback and advice. Thank you.

Yours sincerely,

Tanya Freedman
Director of Jolly Good Art Studio

Your logo and your school name must become familiar to as many people as possible. The more people notice it, recognize it, use it, and talk about it, the more indirect advertising your school receives.

The font and colors of your logo, which includes you name and slogan, should be distinct, vibrant, and recognizable. All the components should work holistically. The Jolly Good Art studio logo is meant to be a symbol of fun, and represent an exclusive, safe place of self-discovery in which children and adults thrive through creative and artistic self-expression. People will encounter your logo whether they come for the short term, such as a one-off birthday party or a charitable event, or they attend a course of lessons or a monthlong summer camp.

An example of effective branding is the website of Loris Lesynski, author, illustrator, and poet. Check it out at www.lorislesynski.com. Her vibrant and fun personality is evident throughout her website, as well as in her business literature and her children's books. This gifted author and illustrator has a reputation for being easy and approachable, and this reputation is captured on her website, which is very interactive. Meeting her confirmed exactly what the website promised, too. (I will share more details about what works so well on Loris's site in Chapter 7.) The overall impression you get from her branding is that what she offers is fun, educational, and interactive. This encourages parents and children to explore and learn more about Loris and her wonderful books.

Advertising works by having a product or service repeatedly on people's minds, on a conscious and subconscious level. We hardly pay attention to the overload of commercials, logos, and brands on TV, radio, and billboards, and in stores all around us. Yet when faced with a huge selection of dishwashing powder or yogurt, we are drawn to a familiar sign or brand, even if we do not know where we recognize it from. The familiar is particularly important when we are attracting students to an art school, and promising fun, education, and safety. In this uncertain world we offer a sanctuary, not just for the creative spirit.

## Marketing Plan

Publicity is just one more tool to sell the "experience" of your unique brand and services. As mentioned earlier, you can never have too much free publicity, as long as it's positive!

Just as market research will help you find out if your ideas are feasible and worthwhile, and just as a strong business plan will help you know where your business is going, a marketing plan will help you figure out the "who, what, where, when, and how" of promoting your business for optimum success.

Even if you offer the best services in the country, it will be a waste of your time and effort if no one is aware of the existence, never mind the uniqueness, of your enterprise.

The marketing plan will equip you with starting points and will help you focus. It will, if done right, teach you whom to approach, and when, where, and how to approach them, so that you can promote your brand — that is, you and your school. Not only will your target audience become aware of your services, but they will be curious and eager to become part of the excitement.

Research books about publicity and apply what you learn. Some of my very favorite books on this subject are listed in the book resources section in the appendix. (I particularly recommend *Getting Publicity* by Tana Fletcher and Julia Roeker, another title by Self-Counsel Press.)

Create your marketing plan by completing the exercises in this chapter. Outline your strategy for reaching your target market, and brainstorm ideas and decide what will suit you and your business best.

It helps not to be shy or modest about yourself or your services. Think of the benefits of what you are offering, and write them down. Your services may help people in many different ways you may not have considered or you have taken for granted.

Schedule one hour a day for publicity-related efforts. Review your short-, medium-, and long-term goals and then translate them into publicity-related actions. Set up a separate filing system for all your publicity folders. Add any article or research you find interesting to a folder and go back to it when you are looking for inspiration. The research you conduct will serve you on many levels while helping you keep current with the news and views of others.

# 7

# CREATING YOUR WEB PRESENCE

*Whether it is a turning point in societal evolution depends not only on the technology — but also how we use it! The web does give us lots more choices about how we organize ourselves.*

— TIM BERNERS-LEE,
FOUNDER OF THE WORLD WIDE WEB

Your website is your unique blueprint — the ever-present Internet business card — with all the necessary up-to-date details of your services to grab hold of the curious prospective client.

This chapter emphasizes the importance of Internet marketing and will help you create an effective website and decide if you will need to hire a professional designer or do it yourself.

## The Importance of Being on the Web

Your website is an integral part of spreading the word about your services. As discussed in Chapter 6, brand awareness — putting your logo and company name in the consciousness of the public — is extremely important. Your distinctive logo and name will be on all your marketing materials — including your website.

At first, many prospective clients will research a business from afar. Going on the Internet, rather than contacting the business directly in person or via telephone, protects people from being cajoled or being asked to commit to something. If they want more information, they would probably email you after seeing your website.

The time and/or money you spend on the design of an extensive website is well worth it. Websites whet the prospective customer's appetite with the promise of outstanding services and fun, unique opportunities for self-discovery and artistic self-expression. A website is yet another way to reach your prospective customer.

I believe there is still much use for "traditional" marketing — the tried and true methods of advertising and promotion — but I see Internet marketing as something that adds a professional edge to your business and streamlines all your efforts. A website address on your promotional literature encourages potential clients to look you up. For example, they may have seen your leaflet promoting a fund-raising event. Your website may well transform their curiosity into actual attendance of your event. They may come up to you for more information and eventually sign up for regular classes.

Another way your website address can come into play is in articles written about your school, whether it is written by you or by someone else. Your own article could have a byline at the end that includes your website address.

By putting your website on as many search engines as possible, you make yourself visible to thousands of prospective customers, even outside your targeted area. The information is available to them seven days a week, 24 hours a day. Ask your web hosting company or a web designer about search engine optimization.

A few years ago I would have gently asked you to consider the benefits of using the Internet in your business. But now I have to ask *when* and *how* you are going to implement a website as part of your business promotion strategy!

If your technical knowledge of the computer and Internet is limited and you do not know where to start, then find out if anyone in your network, including family members, can help you start your website. Teenagers, by the way, are a great source of computer skills.

You will need to decide which route is best for you: hiring a professional web designer or doing it yourself (with the help of templates and technical support). Research web design companies and software before committing money and time to either option. Familiarize yourself with books on web page creation, and what web-hosting packages are available. Try out their templates. Ask around for recommendations on web-hosting companies and what to look out for. I know time is of the essence, but I urge you to set aside time for this research. It is worth it to acquaint yourself with what is entailed in website creation, even if you simply end up hiring a professional web designer.

I used Network Solutions, a US-based web-hosting company. I found their templates for designing a website very helpful and user-friendly. A 24-hour technical support system was included in their hosting package. They also offered their own web design service.

You may also create your own website using programs such as FrontPage and Dreamweaver.

I recommend getting a hit counter too. This helps you know how many people are visiting your site. (It may be included in your web-hosting package.) This is important also because you can see whether a percentage of these people are calling you about your services. There are daily, weekly, or monthly traffic reports that will show you which parts of your site are being visited and how often.

## Important Information to Include on Your Website

What does your business website need to include? It can be highly detailed about your school's programs along with what your school is all about, or it may be a minimal, two-page website that contains the same information as one of your flyers or leaflets.

First impressions are crucial. Think about the few short seconds we give to commercials, or anything or anyone that offers you something. Your site should interest your potential clients within the first few seconds of seeing it. You must appeal to all generations and all levels of artistic talent and experience, and encourage viewers to stay and explore your website and learn about the services you have to offer.

The first page of your site has to be snappy and tell visitors what the site is all about. The Jolly Good Art home page welcomed and thanked readers for visiting, and immediately invited them to click on the topic that most interested them. Get to the point as you only have a short time to convince the visitor you have got the goods they want.

The Jolly Good Art website started off with just five pages. This was plenty for my purposes. I spent two to three weeks learning how to use web page templates and how to upload them, and I also researched other people's websites, and not just other art schools and art-oriented educational sites. What were these sites trying to convey and did they convince me about what they were intending to sell? I discovered that the most effective websites are —

- informative,
- user-friendly,
- easy to navigate,
- well balanced,
- simple in layout and structure,
- aesthetically pleasing, and
- up to date.

The following list includes the things I found important to include on the Jolly Good Art website:

- Description of classes (seasonal and regular)
- Students' artwork
- Mission statement
- An "about us" section that described the commitment of staff, diversity of services, and uniqueness of the school
- Promise of what clients could expect
- Testimonials and photos of happy clients
- Registration forms and surveys for current students
- Newsletters
- Newspaper articles about Jolly Good Art
- Upcoming events
- Business and personal bio

- Description of charity events, including photos

- Links to businesses that advertise my website address on their sites

- Businesses that display my promotional literature or that I partner with for events or promotions (e.g., other schools, doctor's offices, bakeries, frame or art supply stores)

- Links to child-friendly sites that featured art contests

As mentioned, your mission statement should be featured on your website. It needs to be short, but it must tell the readers exactly what your business offers. The following was Jolly Good Art's mission statement:

> *Jolly Good Art's mission is to help people of all ages and backgrounds to discover and express their hidden and vibrant talents by appreciating and creating art.*

Another important feature to include on your website are testimonials from your current and past clients. For example, *"Tanya has a gift for sharing the joy and wonder in art and creativity. Most of all, it's fun!" Signed CG.* (Remember to get permission from your clients.)

I also included a page of my students' artwork. I changed the artwork every month to keep it fresh and to give every student a chance to see his or her work on the site. It also gave their friends and relatives around the world a chance to see their work. (If you decide to do this, make sure to get written permission from the students. If they are underage, you will need their parents' permission as well.) Place captions to the photos with the student's first name and age, and design the website so that when visitors click on the pictures they can see more details such as the title, the subject, and the artistic medium. If you use thumbnails, you can link them to a bigger image with a high resolution. I took pictures of the artwork using my digital camera. Seventy-two dpi or higher is good resolution for a website. Remember that lengthy download times for artwork may deter those who do not have the most up-to-date computer system.

Consider how to keep people interested from the first moment they enter your website. Find out which software package makes it quick and easy to upload images on a regular basis.

On some websites I noticed that publicizing the art and the artists themselves was clearly the priority. I realized this would not be suitable for a school website. On my website, the services came first, and I came last. I did include a few pieces of my own artwork to show where I was coming from. I also compiled a number of special accolades I received as a teacher and director, and I included a short biography for those interested to know more about me. This personal information was on the last page of my site.

Linking to other business sites is a good way to advertise for all those involved. Contact other businesses and tell them of the benefits of being associated with your website, but obviously only if it really does benefit the other business, and vice versa. For example, having links to art supply stores would be handy to your students and potential clients.

I included a news and activities page of upcoming events, such as Craft for Charities events or World Wildlife Fund marathon painting weekends. I also included details of upcoming programs and alerted readers about early registration for art camps.

For the home-based studio, privacy is important. I did not include my home-studio address on my website. The vicinity and town name is sufficient. Your home-based business should not attract passing traffic; instead, you want prospective clients to arrange an appointment.

## Including your prices and registration forms on the website

Depending on whether you want the website to contain complete details or to encourage visitors to phone for these details, you may decide not to include prices. I opted to give prices on my site as I was aware that Jolly Good Art's services were priced competitively. (If some people found the prices too high, I saved them an enquiring phone call.) I highlighted the "early bird registration" and "recommendations" discounts as clear incentives to new and current clients.

In addition to the details about the exclusive art programs planned for the seasonal camps, I included registration forms online. People either sent in their details electronically and mailed the checks, or more frequently, they came to check out the premises and gave me the signed forms and payments personally. Once I received an application, I would immediately put the contact details in my database.

## Should You Design Your Website?

The Internet is the most important advertising and promotional tool of any business. Depending on your technological competence and your budget, you have a choice of either designing your own website (perhaps at the beginning or once you have a broader client base), or having someone else help you or do it all for you for a fee or through a barter arrangement.

As my start-up budget was not large, I decided to create my own website myself. You can save hundreds or even thousands of dollars, depending on how complicated the site will be. I researched what sites I liked and did not like, learned how to use templates, and then created my own site. I instead spent my initial financial resources on better quality art materials and supplies.

There are many advantages to creating your own website. You are in control of all aspects of design and content, and you can update and make any changes instantaneously.

The disadvantages can include your time and resources: you have to spend time acquainting yourself with the technicalities, researching websites, and coming up with your own unique vision and style for your site. Although it is a worthwhile and even enjoyable endeavor, beware of spending too many hours in front of the computer when your time could be spent more profitably elsewhere. Especially at the beginning, you must focus and prioritize. Record how much progress is achieved. You will be surprised at how absorbing and time-consuming creating a website can be.

In my own case, I reasoned that I was an artist with my own vision, and that news about Jolly Good Art would be time-sensitive and I would prefer to do any updates myself. You can still choose to be in control of updates and maintenance even if you get a professional to design your site, but you must be technically competent enough to do so.

In time you may find that your website will evolve to have a personality of its own, which reflects the school's ambience. Eventually the time will come to put more energy into honing it into something even more special.

You may start off by creating a small one-page site that is more of an "introductory calling card," which you can get free from many providers, such as Yahoo! GeoCities. But as you stive to become more professional and to make the right impression with all your communications, you may decide to hand over a redesign to a professional. He or she may be able to breathe completely new life and dimension into your website. Seeing someone else's creative take on your vision may "wow" you.

## Should You Hire a Professional Web Designer?

If, at the beginning, your budget will not allow you to hire a professional, or you would prefer to concentrate on other parts of the business, you should at least network with someone who could eventually help you create a website.

Join forces with someone who is passionate about computers and creating websites. Perhaps he or she can help you as you design and maintain a site yourself. And perhaps you can strike up a bartering agreement, an art class for each computer tutorial.

Once you see the benefits of a bigger website you can justify increasing the time and budget for it.

Whether you are dealing with a designer or a friend, be very clear about your needs and what you expect from him or her. Leave no room for misunderstandings or disappointments by either party, communicating exactly how you imagine the site to look. Bring up several websites you particularly like and do not like. If the designer has listened and communicated with you thoroughly and correctly interpreted your visions, you are practically guaranteed to have a great website. For the money you've spent, you have freed up time to concentrate on other things.

Before signing a contract with a designer, decide who will be responsible for creating and setting up the hosting package, and whether you will maintain your own site after that or if the web designer will update it regularly for you. Ask how long it will take to create the site or make updates. I repeat, communication with the designer is important right from the outset — a lot of money and energy may be wasted otherwise.

The biggest disadvantages of hiring a professional web designer are the time it may take for your updates to be implemented and the expense. The advantages are talent and resourcefulness, which may be well worth the disadvantages.

As the business owner, you know exactly what message you want to give people who visit your website. You still have to compose newsletter copy, scan students' new artwork, and send these files to the web designer for uploading. Remember that you are probably not the designer's only customer, which means you may have to wait for the designer to post your content. This could cause problems if you have a special event coming up soon.

It would be wise for you to learn how to update your site yourself, going beyond the basics so you can be a bit artistic and creative with it.

Ask people in your network to recommend designers. If you can, ask a designer's clients what their experiences were. You need to know if the designer is reliable, timely, and open to suggestions. This is your site, and your ideas need to come before the designer's ideas.

# An Example of a Great Website

As mentioned in Chapter 6, Loris Lesynski's website (www.lorislesynski.com) is a perfect example of a fun, informative, and interactive site that encourages children and parents to stick around and learn more about the author and her books. The website also includes a "what's new" section, as well as ideas for activities, printable pages to color on, writing and drawing information, and content for educators. This is what I think works really well on her website:

- The inviting bright colors.

- A reflection of her approachable and entertaining personality, and her love and passion for books, art, and poetry.

- Inspiring trust and creativity while being informative and educational.

- Her quirky and unique humor (which is the essence of her books and who she is).

- Attractive to adults as well as children. (After seeing this website, a child who loves Loris's books commented, "I feel like I've known her forever.")

- Interactive materials for drawing and poetry.

- Creative ideas for activities.

- The home page button is literally a button!

- Punchy and unique illustrations.

- Links for artists and teachers.

Explore Loris Lesynski's website and other sites to get an idea of what you think is a good website.

Complete Exercise 19, Preparing for a Website.

# EXERCISE 19
# PREPARING FOR A WEBSITE

1.  What do you want your website to say to potential and current clients?

2.  What do you want your website to say about your services and the school as a whole?

3.  What impression do you want your website to make? Number the following factors in order of importance for the impression you want to make:
    _____ Educational
    _____ Fun
    _____ Quirky
    _____ Entertaining
    _____ Inspiring
    _____ Encouraging more curiosity
    _____ Other: _____

4.  Research some of your favorite business websites. What do you like about each site's overall message? What would you do differently?

5.  Do you have the technical knowledge to create your own website? If not, research web designers, ask friends and colleagues for recommendations, and create a short list of designers to contact.

6.  Do you have the writing skills to write the text for your website? If not, who might be able to assist you?

7.  How much time per week can you spend on updating the website?

# 8

# INTERVIEWING AND HIRING EMPLOYEES

*I make progress by having people around who are smarter than I am — and listening to them. And I assume that everyone is smarter about something than I am.*

— HENRY J. KAISER, AMERICAN INDUSTRIALIST

This chapter will help you communicate to employees about your business. It includes information on interviewing and hiring employees as well as creating a contract with your employees.

## Hiring Suitable Staff

We can't do everything ourselves. When you are able to afford them, employing specialists and temporary assistants will make your life easier and be well worth the investment. And you may come to the point where you finally need to take on staff. What are the practicalities of hiring, training, and overseeing staff? What is the difference between organizing and managing yourself and managing others? How do all the personalities in your team work together?

Aim for win-win solutions when dealing with people, whether they are clients, suppliers, or members of your network. The same goes for your staff. To get commitment from your staff, you first need to find the *right* staff. And you must offer them as wonderful a work environment as you can. You must look hard for the perfect fit for you, your business, your classes, and the image you want your school to convey. It is important your employees reflect your ethics and are committed to continual improvement. But remember, no matter how committed your staff may be to your vision, they will not — and should not — be as self-sacrificing as you, the owner of the business.

**119**

## Assistants

Jolly Good Art started small, and I was on my own for the first few months. Eventually I recruited a responsible assistant who helped take the load off of running classes and managing birthday parties. As my business grew and became busier, I employed more assistants as well as other teachers for other special events and for camps. Hiring help freed up my time, enabling me to focus on the bigger picture to keep my business competitive. Jolly Good Art was becoming renowned for its unique and creative programs. I needed time to research, develop, and prepare these programs.

It all started when I asked a mature, fun-loving teenager named Tanya if she would like to help me at the school. I explained what the work would entail and I paid her a higher than average hourly rate. Tanya was very keen and amazingly astute. It was fun to have the extra gimmick of two Tanyas running classes and parties.

Having an assistant took off the pressure of trying to do too much by myself. With the help of the assistant, the parties went smoothly and flawlessly, and the atmosphere was unhurried. After all, the clients were there to have fun.

And what do assistants get out of this? They are getting precious experience with students and with the daily running of a small business. Tanya was a godsend. And I hope the school was a good thing in her life. In addition to her personal achievements in extracurricular activities, her résumé now lists a myriad of duties that she performed during her years at Jolly Good Art. Her knowledge and skills have grown immensely through extensive contact with children.

Sample 9 is a job description that I used to entice potential assistants to work at Jolly Good Art.

A birthday party with 8 to 15 children usually went on for two-and-a-half hours. As mentioned, I paid a higher than average hourly rate. I really appreciated the assistance. The responsibilities would vary slightly for classes and for camps, but the most important rule an assistant had to know about was that everyone had to have fun, fun, and more fun, with a lot of creativity thrown in!

## Teachers

Ask yourself exactly what you need assistance with. You may plan to run classes, birthday parties, and other events throughout the year with student help, and maybe employ specialist teachers for summer camps. (Note that availability may be an issue during the summer.) Or you may decide to take on other teachers to work full time.

The personalities that make up your staff have to click with you and match the school's image. Ideally, after a while of working alongside you, their natural warmth and fresh ideas will come through and will mean a closer bond with you and with the students.

After a reasonable amount of time, you may decide to actually stop teaching classes and have your teachers become the main instructors. You may just want to oversee classes and events from afar, helping out by serving drinks and snacks and replenishing art materials. Make sure you are completely happy that they will inspire the students' and the parents' trust, just the way *you* have over the years.

## SAMPLE 9
# ASSISTANT'S JOB DESCRIPTION

Jolly Good Art has an opening for an assistant to help with birthday parties. The job includes the following duties:

- Prepare art tables with snacks and drinks
- Welcome guests and ensure they wash hands for snack time
- Keep a watchful eye on students and ensure their safety
- Prepare and replenish art materials and supplies for the chosen project
- Help clear projects from art tables
- Assist in serving pizza, drinks, and cake
- Monitor and keep children entertained while cake is being cut and served
- Assist with preparing customized gift bags (e.g., matting the oil pastels for participants)
- Help clean up

Learn to delegate and don't be afraid of hiring teachers who may shine even brighter than yourself. Inspire and mentor them to surpass even you. (Many people only hire those who are not a "threat," whether in terms of intelligence or creative talents.) High-caliber staff who appreciate your leadership and vision are likely to be loyal, dependable, and effective team workers.

In the first years of running the business I made a conscious decision to have realistic expectations from my staff. If you inspire enough dedication, you may not need to crack the whip to get things accomplished! But at the same time, do not anticipate the kind of commitment that you may expect from an equal partner, or someone with a large vested interest in your business. This business is your vision, not theirs. Make it clear what you expect from them, and find ways to keep them constantly motivated. Your staff is there to do the best job they can and leave you with the rest of the responsibilities. If you put too much pressure on them, they may not feel happy to be part of your team.

I was lucky to connect and fuse with eager and committed staff. With 15 years of experience as an executive administrative assistant in London, England, I learned what kind of boss and work environment motivated me most. This later fueled my determination to build a dynamic team of staff in which we supported one another wholeheartedly. It is so important to make one another feel validated with positive feedback. It helps everyone move forward, and creates a nurturing atmosphere.

To build the best team that makes your establishment flourish you should —

- keep your expectations of people realistic,

- pay them as much as you can reasonably afford (i.e., above the going rate), and

- show your appreciation for their extra effort (e.g., giving them gift certificates and treating them to meals).

To recruit good teachers, ask an independent agency or government agency for recommendations. Teachers may also come to you from local schools. Art colleges are another place to look for good teachers — post advertisements on bulletin boards for graduates or students seeking experience.

## Training Your Staff

I kept my expectations realistic, but I also wanted the people I was training (assistants and teachers) to achieve as much success as possible. You must not take it for granted that because you have explained something a few times, it is clear or that your staff will remember what you say. Strive to be patient, approachable, and open to questions and suggestions. Your way may not be the only or best way of doing things.

The extent of training a teacher depends on what role you will give them. Perhaps the teacher will just be a right-hand person in your class, or, after an overlap period in which you work together, you will let them teach their own classes. If you do, you may first want to sit in on classes to see how they are doing. You will also want to gauge the students' reactions to the teacher's style of teaching.

You may want to discuss with the teacher what he or she wants to teach and what you think the course should include, based on your own experience. Respect the teacher's uniqueness and creativity, which will only enhance the school's curriculum.

## Payment

According to some people, I was paying my staff — especially the assistants, who would otherwise earn minimum wage elsewhere — way above the going rate. I resolved this issue in my mind at the outset, having calculated the benefits of high-quality help.

It is true, however, that the money you pay your staff could well be put to other uses, such as on art materials and marketing. It is important to decide exactly how much you are going to pay your staff before you hire anyone. If, after you hire staff, you find that the costs are impinging on the projected profit margins, you must revisit your business plan, recalculate the original pricing structure, and consider increasing the fees for your services.

## Staff Incentives

Encourage your staff's input. You can learn a lot from their ideas, and they will feel respected, valued, and appreciated if you try their suggestions.

When you have a gem of a person who is always there for you, whether an assistant or a regular or seasonal teacher, look after him or her. Perhaps your team will be made up of these gems. Retain your team. These people are the ones who make your establishment a great success and a cut above the competition. Show your staff that you appreciate them by giving them rewards, recognition, perks, and incentives, especially if they provide work that is above and beyond. (They may even provide referrals to new clients.) A special gift for each of your staff at the end of a season or even at unexpected times says so much more than a bonus given grudgingly.

Remember, your employees are your advocates, and yet another link to the community.

# Interviewing

Make a list of the ideal qualities and traits that you would like a staff member to possess before searching for candidates and interviewing them. Jolly Good Art's list started out small and then evolved over time. Consider the following characteristics:

- Mature
- Responsible
- Fun
- Loves working with children (if your school will be teaching children)
- Creative
- Enjoys art
- Patient
- Resourceful
- Honest
- Willing to learn new things
- Accommodating
- Gives positive and constructive feedback to students
- Discreet with students, their parents, and other staff

Read résumés thoroughly, and ask for references and call them. You need to confirm the candidate's traits as seen by other employers.

You also need to find out what the candidate's limitations are, and exactly what skills would be brought to the table, and the diversity of his or her experiences. On a practical level, you must find out hours of availability and how much he or she expects to be paid. These are things you can find out in the actual interview.

When you are ready to compile interview questions, use Form 7 to help you.

I learned early on to depend on my intuition when it came to choosing candidates. The résumé and the references could be perfect, but there could still be something that wasn't clicking between the candidate and me. Some interviewees answer what they think the prospective employer wants to hear, rather than being open and true.

Shortly before the end of a class, I liked to invite the candidates to meet the students and interact with them. This way I could see how the prospective teacher would fit in.

If you want to confirm your impressions before signing a contract with a new teacher, get them to work with you for a few classes or camp days, with other assistants present. If you do hire them, this will also double as their preparation period. The trial period can be a week or even a single session.

Although you may not have a psychology degree or psychic powers, what I believe all creative people and entrepreneurs have is a "gut instinct." With time you will learn to trust and listen to your inner voice. There is no better teacher than experience itself.

# FORM 7
## INTERVIEW QUESTIONS

1. Do you like working with children? Why?

2. What particular aspects of art and different media do you like? Why?

3. How would you describe your teaching style? Please consider the following questions:

    a) Do you teach by the book, with emphasis on artistic structure for students of all ages?

    b) Are you flexible and resourceful according to class and school needs?

    c) Is your style fun and uniquely creative?

    d) Do you use unorthodox methods, such as using unusual materials and subjects to stimulate and develop the artists' minds?

4. In addition to enjoying art, what other qualities do you possess that you could bring to this school?

5. What is your favorite part of being an art or special needs teacher?

6. Where do you envision going with your career in the short, medium, and long term?

7. If you had a young student who obviously did not want to participate in the class, what action would you take so he or she would not distract the class?

8. How would you resolve a dispute among students over which subject to concentrate on for a given session?

9. Would you be able to attend all the scheduled sessions and camp days or do you have any other responsibilities that may make this difficult?

10. What other limitations or constraints do you have?

I once interviewed a very talented graduate student and art teacher who loved working with children. However, something just didn't click. For one thing, the interviewee did not turn off her cell phone during the interview (which kept on ringing every 15 minutes). Despite the feeling that something was not quite right, I offered her the job on a trial basis. She assured me that she was definitely available to start working the following week for the three weeks before the summer camp sessions. She seemed very enthusiastic and said she was grateful for the opportunity to be working at Jolly Good Art.

However, when it came time for her to show up for work, she didn't. She didn't even call to tell me that she wouldn't be joining the company after all. I had been depending on her. Thankfully, I had a contingency plan — I had had the foresight to interview other teachers. Jolly Good Art could not afford to be without the right staff at the busiest periods throughout the year. My gut instinct gets stronger with every experience and now I almost always act on it.

As mentioned in Chapter 1, your prospective employees should also be required to complete a criminal record check before they begin working at your school. You are responsible for the safety of your students and this is one more way to make sure you are protecting them.

# Employee Contract

When you hire an employee, you may want to create a signed contract. This will decrease the chance of miscommunication about what you expect from each other. Keep the original copy of the contract and give the employee a copy, or create two originals that you both sign.

The contract should be written clearly and include the following information:

- What the program will offer and entail
- Duties and responsibilities expected from both you and the employee
- Wage and information about wage increases

- Hours of work and break times

- What materials will be provided by you and/or the employee

- Assurance of safety of staff and students

- Should the employee terminate employment, he/she will not start an art establishment within a five-mile radius of the school

Communication is paramount. From the beginning be very clear about the responsibilities so everyone, including you, will know what they have to do and when. Take into consideration what each employee is good at, his or her long-term goals and aspirations, and how to make this alliance run as smoothly as possible. You are depending on your staff so that you can pursue other aspects of your business. (Just make sure you do not become overly dependent on them.)

## Safety for Employees and Students

The most important thing you have to consider is the security and safety of those in your care, and those you employ should you have assistants and teachers.

I was determined to hire people who were not only responsible and enjoyed being around children but who also had first-aid qualifications. If possible, all your staff should know CPR and have first-aid training. You never know when the Heimlich maneuver will become necessary.

During summer camps, consider that recreational times include indoor and outdoor games. How many teachers and assistants will you need to supervise the students? You need to prepare your staff for

the little accidents that may occur, such as a scraped knee or elbow, but also for more serious situations such as an allergic reaction to a bee sting.

Everyone should know where the first-aid kit is, including the students. Your staff should also know exactly what is in the first-aid kit, which I suggest should include the following:

- Polysporin or any other antibiotic cream

- Sterile adhesive bandages in assorted sizes

- Gauze pads and roller bandages

- Tweezers

- Scissors

- Antiseptic

- Antihistamine lotion for relief from bug bites

- Latex gloves

- Sunscreen

- Thermometer

- Nonprescription drugs (e.g., aspirin or other pain reliever, antidiarrheal medication, antacid)

Your staff and students should also know what to do in case of a fire. There should be maps around the studio showing everyone what exits to use in case of an emergency. You should also discuss with your staff the procedure of evacuating students safely.

As mentioned in Chapter 3, the registration form (Form 2) includes a section for allergies and medical issues. The more prepared you are, the better you can deal with an emergency.

**9**

# NETWORKING

*Asking costs little.*

— ITALIAN PROVERB

In this chapter we discuss the need for effective networking as well as how you can help the community by volunteering and mentoring.

## What Is Networking?

Networking means different things to different people. Generally speaking, networking means opening up new horizons on a business or personal level. (Business and personal networking often overlap.) Successful networking means asking for and getting what you need from the people around you. In turn you should learn to give generously to those in your social and business circles.

A network widens your range of personal contacts and has the effect of generating more business. Networking simply makes business sense. You pursue new avenues and cultivate more contacts. Joining a group formed around the same interest or hobby is not only a fun way to spend your time — it's also a great way to network.

My hobbies include art, travel, writing, and cooking. In the process of pursuing these hobbies, my love of art and writing in particular has become more focused. I've had the opportunity to be in social settings with new people as well as with like-minded friends.

Is there anything that may be holding you back? Are you too shy, too busy, or too afraid to come across as being aggressive? Think about the areas in which you could improve, then take action. Maybe a group like Toastmasters can help you.

## Why Network?

In addition to the advantages to your business, you may want to be a part of a support or networking group simply to give you a sense of belonging. But mainly, being active in various groups opens up new opportunities, and it benefits your business in ways that are both tangible and intangible.

The tangible benefits include direct leads and industry information that may be of instant help to your business. For example, you could find financial backing or a partner to help run your business. The intangible benefits include benefits to future scenarios. Perhaps someone you meet now will eventually become a client or will refer others. Another intangible benefit is emotional support — you may develop new relationships full of trust and respect.

You are taking a sincere interest in other individuals and learning from their points of view, how they think, and their vision — perhaps they have a business of their own. We can all glean something new. Perhaps a chartered accountant you meet gives you advice during a coffee break at a networking event, and she sheds light on a dilemma you have been trying to figure out for the past few months. (Your own accountant may have been too close to interpret your current issue objectively.)

The Internet is a necessary tool when it comes to networking. You keep the lines of communication open, via email and your website, not only with prospective clients, but with colleagues, mentors, and everyone you work with. And you participate in discussion boards online and get information from people around the world.

An example of networking I'd like to share with you: Heather Skoll runs a yoga school, which my daughter has attended for a few years. Heather is the mother of special needs children, and has also had experience with special needs children through work. I had read articles profiling her amazingly diverse personal and professional life and gotten to know her personally. Witnessing her help her children progress in the mainstream educational system has been gratifying and inspirational. She has a passion for teaching, and she imparts a Zen-like wisdom. She has strengthened my respect and understanding of children with special needs and those who help them.

## Ask for What You Need

Ask for what you need from others and you may be pleasantly surprised and abundantly rewarded. Many successful entrepreneurs have said to me that they would be more than happy to pass along their own experiences and lessons learned — if only they were asked. Too often new entrepreneurs are shy and afraid they will come across as too aggressive, needy, or naïve. Ask yourself what is the worst that can happen. Are you afraid that the person you are asking for help will refuse? It is rare that someone will refuse to give advice. If anything, he or she may ask you to reschedule to a better time.

As mentioned in Chapter 1, make sure that if you ask for 20 minutes for an information interview, you keep it to 20 minutes. This shows respect. Make sure you send a card or a short email thanking the person for his or her help.

Gauge if this person can help you further, and be clear with your request. Many people appreciate my directness, and they seem to like precise requests with deadlines. I have found that my close friends admire my forwardness and have even taken a page from my book.

If you are asking something from close pals or your family, you will know from their initial response whether or not you are being reasonable, and they will probably be honest about what and how much they can help you with your business.

Be resourceful and think outside the box (and beyond). You can only be as successful as you allow yourself to be. Learn to see every person you meet, no matter where you meet them, as a prospective customer or as someone who knows a prospective customer.

My friend and mentor, Donna Messer, is a networking guru. Her horizons are boundless, and her motto is "how can we help you?" She lives up to her promise of putting people in touch with one another. Just like Donna, I strongly believe in Stephen Covey's "abundance mentality" discussed in his book *The 7 Habits of Highly Effective People* (Free Press, 2004). There is plenty of success for everyone out there — generosity leads to abundance. Do not be stingy with what you can offer, including your own knowledge and what you are learning along the way. Share your passions and dreams, and listen to others'.

If no one knows about your business and your plans, no one can advocate them for you. This is not the time to be modest and hope for the best. Be clear about what your business offers, making sure people know enough about your services to feel comfortable enough to recommend them.

Network with your family, friends, and acquaintances and mine for relationships that will be mutually advantageous. Ask if anyone knows someone who would benefit from your services. For example, perhaps a colleague of yours seems to be quite a keen networker, but none of his family members, to whom he could recommend your school's services, live locally. So you ask if his friends or neighbors would be interested (and perhaps they have artistic children or spouses). You mention the benefits that adults, as well as children, gain from discovering art, and leave it to the person to connect the remaining dots.

Be specific. For example: "Do you know of anyone locally who may be interested in art classes, birthday 'art' parties, or seasonal art camps?"

If someone in your network doesn't know anyone to recommend your services to, offer your business card and ask them to think of you when, and if, anyone comes to mind later. Return the favor if they have a business to promote — mutual help for fellow entrepreneurs. Keep their details, check out their website if they have one, acquaint yourself with their services and products, and keep your eyes and ears open for ways to help them.

# Networking Is a Two-Way Street

You can search for and seize opportunities, but just as importantly, networking is a two-way street. Do not get a reputation as a "freeloader." Ask for help, but do not become a nuisance. Leave it to others to support and recommend you.

Make the effort to be there for your close friends. They are your lifeline throughout the beginning, the middle, and — if you should wish to sell your business — the end.

Actively listen to what people want, whether parents think there is a missing component in the school's curriculum, or a businessperson is looking for referrals for his or her bookkeeping or frame-making business. We all know more people who can help each other than we think. See it in terms of "six degrees of separation": We are all connected in this small world, and everyone, no matter where they are, can be reached through a short chain of six (or fewer) social acquaintances.

Dig deeper to figure out exactly what you want and how you can help others. Mutual networking is about helping and supporting each other. What is the incentive to work on your behalf and promote your business?

Gain experience with a business before you refer them. When I need to have my art or my students' art framed, I may go to my new contact with a small order so I can form an opinion on their quality and price. If I am happy to be associated with this company, I may agree on a discount deal for my students for bulk orders.

The bartering system works well in two-way networking. For example, you may know someone who can look after your children in return for the same — or you can pay this person with art lessons he or she has always wanted but could not afford. Or you may meet a bookkeeper with whom you could arrange a mutually beneficial situation.

In addition to mentoring students, your staff, and those who ask for entrepreneurial guidance, there are many ways that you can "pay back." For example, sometimes parents would ask me to display catalogs or brochures of their wares or services (e.g., yoga, dance), or charity draws. If you have a genuine desire to help others, you will find the opportunities and they will find you. Just think broadly and be generous. Some wonderful things have happened for me and I have been rewarded in many more ways than I could have imagined.

## Volunteering

Volunteering, that is, offering your time and expertise to the community, has many advantages. If it appears impossible to take time out of your already overtaxed days and weeks, just consider the many benefits you may reap. Not only will it be personally rewarding, but you may also discover opportunities that you had not expected. In the long run, volunteering will pay you in many more ways than you ever imagined.

Pay attention to exactly what others would like from you. Listening takes practice and commitment, as well as finding the opportunities to help, especially if you are dogmatically focused on your own business.

Here are some suggestions as to where to volunteer:

- Public or school libraries
- Charity organizations including those that arrange "walk for causes" and other events

- Craft fairs
- Special needs groups
- Hospitals
- Retirement homes
- Churches
- After-school programs in public or private schools and at local community centers

In addition to making a difference, you are getting to know people and becoming part of the community. You can also become aware of the concerns of the community.

Your helpfulness and willingness to give time to volunteer will earn you a reputation as a strong, kind, and generous member of the community. People will see you — in business and in your personal life — as a sincere, giving person, who helps others. This will encourage loyalty, and people will make time for you and recommend your services to others wholeheartedly.

If you are the type of person who gets excited about helping, but feels that others sometimes take advantage of you, take heart. Be aware of your generosity and be assertive at the same time. Yes, there is always a need for willing helpers, but prioritize your business and personal needs, and weigh the benefits of volunteering and mentoring. Of course, ignoring your business priorities could cause problems and dilemmas, so learn to prioritize and when to say no. (There is more on this topic in Chapter 10, Get Organized and Stay Organized.)

## Reputation

I particularly enjoy inspiring and helping children. Parents of children with special needs told me they appreciated how Jolly Good Art did not label their kids, but treated everyone as unique and individual artists. They were helped according to their understanding of the art medium.

Be the kind and caring person you wish others to be and the right people will come into your life and business. Cultivate a reputation as someone who has integrity, keeps promises, and is trustworthy — as a member of the community your reputation is crucial. It also grows with time. Especially in a small town, your establishment will soon become a familiar brand in your neighborhood.

## Finding or Creating a Networking Group

The larger the organization or group you belong to, the more dynamic it can be for networking. The diversity of personalities and level of closeness and helpfulness among the members vary from group to group, of course. In most cases, established groups are more vibrant, and the energy within them is ever-changing.

Cliques will form no matter where you go, and bonds forged may become stale and stagnant. Beware that some groups may actually stunt your growth or undermine you unintentionally. Be very selective who you surround yourself with.

Groups to look for can include those for parenting, small-business entrepreneurs, writing or reading, or for whatever your passions may be. If you don't find anything, consider starting your own. Creating a group will help you develop new friendships faster than if you just joined an existing group. But keep in mind that you cannot afford to digress and divert too much of your attention from your business. If you are like me and are sometimes driven to doing too many things, remind yourself that you are cultivating a "networking pasture" to enhance your business and personal life. Stay focused and organized, otherwise you will find yourself with one extra project to juggle among your many other responsibilities. No matter how attractive or fun the endeavor of starting the best networking club may appear, it can take away a lot of your time and energy.

But what if the benefits far outweigh the costs? For example, a support group run for and by single working parents may be far away in the next town. Starting your own such group may be the best option.

Allocate an appropriate amount of time to this project and stick to the schedule. Do not hesitate to ask for committed members to take on some of the responsibilities. Although it is gratifying to form a group (it is, after all, a support system in which everyone has a lot to gain), your family and your business should be your first priorities. List the strengths, challenges, opportunities, and threats (SCOT analysis) to clarify how your needs can be best met without cutting into your down time.

If the members of your group are gregarious and everyone appears to get a lot out of the meetings, a meeting every week or two weeks may be a good idea. Keep the momentum going.

The mission of people in a networking group should always be to support one another. Whether it is to help you become a better negotiator, parent, or communicator, keep in mind what you need from your group as well as how you can help others.

Take, for example, the professional speaking support organization Toastmasters International as mentioned in Chapter 2. Their mission is to help members achieve personal development and success and forge a strong network. Each individual chapter has 20 to 30 members. This tried-and-true system is very successful. It takes into account that everyone has his or her own individual goals and progresses at his or her own pace.

Here are some examples of social networks. The list includes groups you can find on the Internet. Although not as effective as a group that meets face to face, they can still be valuable sources of information and support, and you can connect with people across the planet:

- *Family*: parents, widows, caregivers of relatives

- *Background*: multicultural, religious, educational

- *Hobbies*: quilting, painting, writing, photography

- *Technical or electronic*: computers, radios, planes, cars

- *Health and healing*: weight management, diseases and disorders

- *Caregiving*: support and care for people with special needs

- *Career and business*: professional speaking, sales-oriented associations, rotary clubs, career development and training

Although many networking groups concentrate on the last category, business, the groups in the other categories can benefit you immensely. I have met many of my close friends through my love of art and writing, in addition to making valuable contacts through business circles. Business and personal interests can certainly overlap; I have had business dealings with some of my friends, and I have learned from and shared invaluable tricks of the trade with both friends and associates.

In addition to the exercises in Chapter 3, Exercise 20 delves deeper into finding or creating the right networking group for you.

# Combining Forces

Combining forces with those who are willing to partner with your art school may be immensely helpful, even if it's just for certain projects. Although many partnerships do not always work out for the best, if you establish common goals and are prepared to work together, to compromise, and to keep it professional, you can definitely reap many rewards. You can learn from each other's expertise, and both of your businesses can gain more exposure and attract new clients.

You may consider partnering with another business to offer classes and art camps in your own studio or theirs, or partnering for a special occasion, a fund-raising event, or an art demonstration. You and your partner should consider how well your programs merge and complement each other. Perhaps you are partnering with a swimming school, with swimming in the morning and the art camp in the afternoon.

Other unique partnerships you could consider are with a bakery or patisserie, cooking school, dance school, or karate school. Ask people in your network if they would be interested in partnering up. You may be surprised at how well it works out, as both your businesses diversify and the local area becomes aware of your services. It is a win-win situation. Keep in mind, however, that everyone has different personalities, visions, and goals, and that everything should be spelled out between you and the other business.

## Creating a contract for partnership programs and events

You and the other business should create a simple and clear contract that includes the following information:

- What the programs will offer and entail

- What is expected from both parties

- What resources are needed, who will be providing them, and what the costs will be

- What venue will be used and at what time

- How the various programs will be organized

- If food will be provided for the event, who will provide the food and dishes

- The cost of the staff and who will pay their wages

Come to an agreement at the beginning — in writing — so there are no misunderstandings or breakdowns of communication. (An agreement between Jolly Good

## EXERCISE 20
# FINDING A NETWORKING GROUP

1. List all the interests that you have ever wanted to pursue. Do not let the constraints of time, money, or energy stand in your way. Are there organizations in your area that cater to any of your hobbies or interests (e.g., photography clubs, runners' groups, etc.)?


2. Would you prefer to meet face to face with other people with similar interests or would you like the support of a virtual community on the Internet?


3. How often (e.g., weekly, biweekly, or monthly) do you want to meet with these people?


4. Would you prefer to join a pre-existing group or start your own?


5. What direct or indirect benefits will you gain from joining a group (e.g., personal development, health improvement, fun, creativity, enhancing your business)?


6. What is holding you back? Number the following factors in order of importance and add your own to the list:
   _____ Time
   _____ Money
   _____ Fear of rejection or embarrassment
   _____ Concern over getting distracted
   _____ Inability to prioritize
   _____ Inability to see the benefits of joining a networking group
   _____ Fear of spending too much time doing things for the group
   _____ Other: _____

Art and Trinity Swim School is provided as a sample on the CD-ROM.) This may be a lucrative future alliance, so do not cut corners and make the mistake of not drawing up a contract. Many good friendships have gone bad because of too much timidity about this at the beginning.

When brainstorming with a partner, the number one focus should be the interest level and demand for the programs, as well as providing diverse stimulation for the clients. You are forging an alliance to offer clients even more choice. Use your imagination and ingenuity, let ideas pop into your head, and listen to all suggestions. Work together and open the door for joint ventures in the future.

## Mentoring and Coaching

If all you can afford are a few short spurts of time networking, then consider mentoring or seeking a mentor. Connecting with people this way can be done easily and conveniently via email. It may give you a much-needed respite without distracting you too much from your plan. You may need help from those you admire and respect who can objectively point you in the right direction, and you can do the same for others. Mentorship can help both the protégé as well as the mentor.

There has to be a connection of values and ethics between mentor and protégé for the relationship to be effective, dynamic, and long-term. In the beginning of your business you need as much help as you can get, whether this is to learn entrepreneurial tricks of the trade or how and where to get financial assistance, emotional support, and networking opportunities. You will gain a tremendous amount from enlisting the services and help of a coach or mentor.

Using sports as an analogy to differentiate between coaching and mentoring, Ian Kennedy, of the consulting firm Essential Communications, says, "The coach is paid, while the team captain is essentially the mentor, and is not paid as such."

Kennedy's company offers coaching and mentoring to individuals at the conceptualizing and strategizing stages. His company helps entrepreneurs and other business leaders in the corporate world to remain aligned with themselves and their goals as they deal with challenges and overcome obstacles.

Over time, the mentor-protégé relationship can sometimes change and evolve into a mutually beneficial one. Kennedy relates the story of working with a colleague for many years and helping her define and own her market niche. Recently she had come to him to offer leads and advice that really helped out his firm.

Mary Lou Di Paolo, a certified coach who services clients in both the corporate and entrepreneurial worlds, shares her definitions of coaching and mentoring:

> Coaching is a partnership between two people with the intention of achieving a goal faster, better, and more efficiently. The "coachees" leave the relationship enriched and empowered to generate results having learned more about themselves from three perspectives: being, doing, and having. "Being" refers to the personal qualities and characteristics people bring to what they "do"

or the actions they take, in order to "have" or produce the results they want.

Mentoring is a partnership between two people that is based on an affinity for one another or a mutual respect. The more "seasoned" of the two people shares his or her personal experiences and may provide advice or counsel. The learning for the more junior person comes from discovering what has been done in the past. The mentor teaches by telling and sharing, unlike the coach who empowers by asking powerful questions and teaching the "client" to fish. The mentor takes the "mentoree" fishing and may actually do the work himself or herself pointing out what to do and how.

## Benefits of hiring a mentor or coach

It does depend on your specific needs at the pivotal points in your enterprise (e.g., at the conceptualizing, start-up, and running stages), as well as the personality types involved, but I believe you can gain greatly from having a coach or mentor.

My relationship with my friend Donna Messer began when I wanted to learn from her networking expertise. This was in the first year of my previous business, importing English antiques. My goals were set and tangible. What I didn't expect was how a friendship would bloom. She understood my ambitions implicitly, and over the years, in

our meeting of minds, the line between "Donna the mentor and coach" and "Donna the friend" (who is always there for me) blurred and became secondary. A bond between two driven people grew.

Donna was someone I truly respected and aspired to learn from on many levels. Without being aware of it, I soon applied lessons I learned from Donna. Specifically, she taught me how storytelling educates and entertains, and also how it can emphasize an important point. (The cycle continues as I mentor others. I will discuss this later on.)

Professional coaches and mentors charge in the range of $60 to $100 per hour, depending on whether it is for one-on-one coaching, for a small business enterprise, or a corporate contract. These professionals are paid to help you, so pinpoint exactly what you need help with and you will get the most out of your relationships, over the short and long term. This is equally important if you consult with someone on a more informal basis who you do not pay.

The right coach or mentor can give a huge boost at the start. He or she may even become a long-term friend whose values and wisdom you combine with your own.

Do you need someone in your corner to help you with tactics and how to be practical and set things up? Or do you need someone to be more of a holistic adviser/ counselor to help you look at the bigger picture?

It is not quite enough to find someone who will merely give you advice or his or her opinions. Ideally, you want to cultivate a mutually rewarding relationship that stays with you indefinitely. You are not looking for someone to rescue you, but someone you can share with and learn from. You want to be guided by someone who understands your business visions and knows what it takes to reach your goal.

As you get to know each other, you must find ways to show your appreciation for his or her time (perhaps by helping him or her in the future), or you must "pay it forward" by mentoring protégés of your own.

To paraphrase Laura Whitworth from her book *Co-Active Coaching* (Davies-Black Publishing, 2007): Imagine someone listening not only to your words, but also to what is behind them — who listens to the spaces between the words … someone in tune with the nuances of your voice, your emotion, your energy, and who listens to the very best in you, even when you cannot hear it yourself.

There are many benefits to hiring a mentor or coach. The *financial* benefits include the following:

- Costly mistakes may be avoided, as well as having to discover things by trial and error.

- You will be encouraged to consider different options and to go for the one best suited to your individual needs and budget.

- A mentor or coach will understand a situation that may be new to you. He or she may have been there before, and can help you progress faster with more certainty.

The *emotional* benefits include the following:

- You will realize that you are not alone on this journey.

- A mentor or coach will provide you with a sounding board and supportive advice.

- A mentor or a coach is skilled and will help you make wise and well-thought-out decisions.

## Finding a coach or mentor

There are many places you can find mentors and coaches. You will find them as you network and do the following:

- Attend industry events

- Seek recommendations from people you trust

- Approach someone you respect in a specialized field

- Join independent business associations

Hiring a coach or a mentor may not be for everyone, but it may be a good investment if this is your first business venture. Exercise 21 will help you decide if this is something you want to explore further. Consider your answers and think about your requirements and budget. This is a big commitment, so do not rush into your decision. If the spark is not quite there between the two of you, don't stop looking. There is a lot of help out there. Do not shortchange yourself or settle for second best.

## You as a mentor and coach

As the owner of a service-oriented business, you will come into contact with many people of all ages with diverse personalities and

# SHOULD YOU HIRE A COACH OR MENTOR?

1. How will you know if a potential coach or mentor will be a good fit for you?


2. What level of experience does the potential coach or mentor have in your business field?


3. How much does this person charge for his or her services?


4. How often do you want to meet with the coach or mentor, and for how long do you expect to continue seeing him or her?


5. Can you afford the services of a coach or mentor now, or can this decision be deferred until later?


6. Will this investment be worthwhile in the long run?

needs. People will be looking up to you as an art teacher and as a boss. Students will need assurance about their artistic talent and self-esteem, and staff members will look to you for supervision. You have the opportunity to positively influence and impart your expertise to those around you. The responsibility is large and satisfying.

And along the way, young entrepreneurs may come up to you and request that you be their mentor. There are some wonderful advantages to being a mentor and coach. Not only do you learn as you teach, it is rewarding and emotionally satisfying to help others, empathizing, listening, and finding ways for your protégé to find his or her own unique talents and solutions. I must admit it is also gratifying to receive recognition in the community and business world for being a person who shares his or her knowledge.

As you gain confidence and experience, you will become a role model for your students and staff. Mentoring will reward you professionally and personally.

# 10

# GET ORGANIZED AND STAY ORGANIZED

*Clutter is postponed decisions.*

— BARBARA HEMPHILL, AUTHOR OF
*TAMING THE PAPER TIGER AT WORK*

In this chapter, you will discover how to get and stay organized by using time management tools and filing systems that work for your personality type and organizational style. This chapter will also help you find a balance for your business and personal life and, most importantly, to recognize signs of burnout.

## Getting Organized

Getting organized will free up precious time, translating to increased productivity and confidence. How you manage your time can make or break your business. Do you put off filing until the pile becomes a mini-wall? Does a friend call for long chats during business hours? Each of us falls prey to ineffective use of time out of habit or because it is so easy to procrastinate.

We have to look at how your organizational style affects the way you manage your time. First, you need to think about how you do things currently and where you need to improve. From there you can assess which time management tools would be best.

There are countless options out there for you to choose from. You may be familiar with the many workshops and books dedicated to this very subject. Effective time management requires diligence, patience, and common sense. Regularly assess what is working and what is not so that you can make necessary adjustments to your routine.

## Organizational styles

Before getting into the nitty-gritty of how you manage your time, let us look into the many different styles of managing your life. (The techniques of time management and organization are as diverse as our own individual personalities.) Look at your attitude, how you perceive and solve problems, your readiness to change and adapt, and your commitment to your goals, including your business.

Find better ways to mitigate the energy sapping, time-consuming tasks, and to maximize your productivity both in the business and outside of it. If your current system is not working, it's time to increase self-discipline, replace self-defeating habits, and find a realistic system that will work in the short and long term.

Which type of organizer are you? Do you prioritize according to what must be finished immediately or to what you enjoy the most? Do you procrastinate? Do different circumstances bring out different behavior? Sometimes time pressures and external stresses make us revert to older, ineffective habits.

You may zigzag among the following styles:

- The *fire starter*, who is a creative soul
- The *plodder*, who is cautious and methodical
- The *convert*, who has evolved from the preceding extremes to become a grounded, dynamic, and successful businessperson

## The fire starter

Many entrepreneurs start off this way, over-enthusiastic, excitable, and maybe a bit crazy, and blaming the creative spirit for their behavior. Too many fingers in too many pies can mean getting easily distracted and going off on tangents. Fire starters have great energy at the beginning of a project, and then they either get bored or overwhelmed. They do not know what to do when things get too complicated. They seek instant gratification, instead of taking a step back and looking realistically and patiently at their goals and how to achieve them. Their goal setting and organizational skills may not be effective. They may keep their ideas in their heads until too many of them accumulate — and they may never be acted upon.

The positive aspects of a fire-starter personality:

- Innovative ideas inspire enthusiastic responses from clients
- Quick to go into action with a "can do" attitude
- Generates positive excitement in staff, clients, and protégés and inspires their commitment
- Fun, spontaneous, creative, unorthodox, and can think outside the box

The negative aspects:

- Disorganized, with too many new ideas bubbling over
- Impulsive
- Despite best intentions, will not always deliver

- May not see a project through to the end due to impractical goal setting

- May tend to be a generalist and not patient enough to specialize

### The plodder

Although being methodical may seem like a positive trait for an entrepreneur, the inflexibility of this personality may be detrimental to a business. Especially if they are involved in a creative enterprise in which innovative, dynamic ideas have to flow and inspire clients and staff.

This perfectionist, by-the-book type will usually get to the finish line eventually. But how many opportunities will be lost along the way? In our fast-paced world where action wins over slow and steady progress, there always has to be a balance between thoroughness and efficiency. Staid and out-of-date techniques will leave clients no choice but to vote with their feet.

Are you a methodical, organized businessperson, but need to learn to do things more effectively? Then start by getting help from those around you, whether they are friends or from your network. Who do you admire that may help you shed your old attitudes? Like getting rid of unsuccessful habits and old administrative systems, you need to learn about different approaches and cultivate effective habits.

The positive aspects of being a plodder:

- Cautious, diligently researching the market and competition, and carefully planning art programs

- Thinks through every step

- Keeps promises (e.g., makes follow-up calls to current and prospective clients)

- Determined to succeed and finish the project

- Aims at perfection and delivering the best possible product and service

- Reliable and is there for his or her peers

- Listens well and would make a great mentor

The negative aspects:

- Overly cautious and set in his or her ways — does not like change

- Inflexible or out of date; may be too conventional, sticking to tried-and-true methods

- May be perceived as unapproachable by various age groups and cultures

- May be uncomfortable with interacting with, and sharing his or her vision with others

- By the time he or she gets to the end result, he or she may have lost potential clients to the competition

### The convert

The convert evolves from either of the above extremes. Having weighed the possibilities of losing business or opportunities because of disorganization or inflexibility, they see the necessity of change.

Depending on the situation and our stress level, we can act like a fire starter or a plodder, or sometimes a bit of both. Be prepared to learn and develop new skills and get out of your comfort zone. Start with what you obviously have challenges with. Ask those who will give you an honest opinion or advice, and use the SCOT analysis.

## The bigger picture

You can never be too busy to get organized. Otherwise your business venture may be doomed.

Are you an early bird who catches all the juicy worms? Or are you a night owl who prefers the peace and silence of the dark hours when the rest of the world does not distract you? Look broadly at how you work, so you can organize your business, yourself, and your family life. They all have a dramatic influence on one another. Once you know what drives you, you can make informed decisions.

While my husband may have hundreds of activities booked in his calendar and in his head, he has got it all under control. Because of the constant juggling and meeting of deadlines that characterize his people-oriented career — he is the director of pharmaceutical research and development for a multinational company — burnout is a real risk. But he has derived an attitude based on Dale Carnegie's classic book, *How to Stop Worrying and Start Living* (Pocket Books, 1990). My husband treats each day in "day-tight compartments." He allocates time in hours, or even 15-minute increments — but uses this only as guidance, not an exact curriculum. He creates a chart to introduce structure into his day and organizes accordingly, but he is still prepared for inevitable interruptions.

In your own business, outward and inward calm is very important. It not only gives the right impression to your clients and staff, you conserve energy by spending it wisely.

Start a routine. Spend one morning a week planning the week ahead, and part of your night planning the next day. Prioritize activities and chores in order of importance, carrying over those tasks you have not yet achieved. Check things off as you complete them so that instead of negatives nagging at your subconscious, you have some sense of accomplishment — this will keep you motivated. It will soon become second nature. Get help with time management challenges and take control. You have a business to run with no time to waste.

From someone who still struggles to keep organized, my advice is to try and keep the papers on your desk to a minimum. They tend to pile up and multiply. I use an upright open filing system to quickly file away new mail and other documents I get constantly. I find it easier to concentrate when my desk is clear.

## Finding the right system

Planning and thinking about how to organize and manage your time is as important as actually implementing a system and sticking to it. You must find the system that works for you. Remember, you can learn from others. Ask what they do to get organized.

Give a trial period of three weeks for any new system you are considering. Twenty-one days is the magic number to form a habit in our psyche. At least you can see if it matches your organizational and time management style and encompasses your business needs. If your previous system was not working out, this new one does not have to be earth shatteringly different or complex, just not more of the same.

If you really cannot get on with the new method within the first few days, and you are really sure it's not for you, then try something else. Be flexible and use your intuition but learn to measure your system's success by ticking off tangible and realistically set goals you set on a daily, weekly, and monthly basis. This may take some time to get used to if it is not in your nature.

Change and adaptability are not always easy, but the effort will be worth it in the long run. Not only for you, but for your clients, your staff, and your family. Design a structure that works for you. Even young children can help. Make it fun and reward them accordingly; for example, "More bedtime reading for helping Mummy with the clearing up of toys."

Accept that you are not a superhuman, and let your family help. Discuss with them how they can lend a hand. They may surprise you.

## Time Management

Do not confuse being busy with being productive. The more successful you become the more you will realize how precious your time is. Your time has to be managed, and learning three principles — *organizing*, *prioritizing*, and *delegating* — will give you more control so you do not get bogged down with the overwhelming demands of your business.

Keep a close eye on where you are spending too much time. Look at where and what the time thieves are in your work life and personal life. Here are some major time thieves:

- Telephone
- Email and Internet
- Family
- Friends and network groups
- Housekeeping
- Entertainment

I cut down on reading and writing emails, both business and personal, disciplining myself to only check and answer email twice a day — first thing in the morning and late in the afternoon.

I answered the business phone, but my friends and family learned to keep social calls to a minimum, respecting my working hours. I scheduled two mornings a week to catch up on filing, administration duties, and nonurgent phone calls. You have a work ethic, and people have to respect that.

Patricia Ruhl is a good friend whom I respect, admire, and learn from constantly. Patricia is a writer and communicator with a special interest in marketing issues. She has held senior communications positions in the financial industry and today works as a freelance copywriter, managing a business and raising her children. The following is Patricia's take on time management:

> Time can be a very elusive concept. It can pass equally quickly or slowly depending on the task. When starting a business I discovered only one speed — fast, that is, barely enough hours in the day to absorb all there is to know. That being said, it's an incredibly exhilarating experience. Managing

time from the outset makes sense. How do you fit everything in? Very simply, plan it. Sit down once a day, either at night or first thing in the morning and think out the necessary tasks. It takes some discipline, but it's well worth it.

Staying on task is another important time management principle. Being focused requires practice. When I started my business I'd set the microwave timer to keep me on track. If I was tempted to look out the window I'd catch myself, knowing the timer was still ticking. It worked surprisingly well!

As far as being flexible, I don't try to manage every moment of the day. Other things are going on in life that are every bit as, or more important than, my business. When those things come up I don't ignore them.

Getting balance is enjoying the challenge of business while attending to the details of life.

To gain control over your business and personal life, first get a handle on time management and perfect your self-discipline. Getting organized is all about managing yourself, your business, and the situations you are in, and time management is an integral part of it.

We all sometimes feel overwhelmed or overstressed, and self-discipline flies out of the window despite our best intentions. Perhaps your mentor or trusted friend can help you analyze your time management. Question how you prioritize and the impact on your business and personal life. Praise yourself for any positive changes you make, and stay proactive, creating new goals, rules, and routines. Relearning the basics of self-discipline will reward you.

## Organize, prioritize, and delegate

In order to manage your time effectively, you need to organize your activities and chores, prioritize these in order of importance, and delegate some of them to others.

Consider the following to help save you time:

- Hire domestic help to clean your home (every two weeks or monthly).

- Make extensive shopping and errand lists (including menus for the week).

- Stick to a routine timetable.

- Prepare double or triple the amount of meals, which can be frozen until needed on busy nights. (This will also save on take-out meals, and is healthier.)

- If you live with a family, create a list of chores that each member can complete.

You will find that prioritizing your tasks will dramatically eliminate all those hours you spend "spinning your wheels." Decide what goes under the following categories: 1) urgent; 2) important but not urgent; and 3) not so important.

You need to ask yourself what is the worst that can happen if the task is not done immediately. Sample 10 will help you understand the categories.

## SAMPLE 10
## CATEGORIZING MY TASKS

*Urgent*
- Prepare a proposal for a prospective client who you promised to call in the next few days.
- Pay the bills that are due right away.
- Do the grocery shopping because there is no food left! Must get done today because of the other commitments of the next few days.

*Important but not urgent*
- Pay the bill that's due in the next few days.
- Catch up on filing.
- Stock up on a specific paint color or materials for next week's project.
- Tidy house before arrival of guests this weekend.

*Not so important*
- Sort out the pile of magazines, frames, and clothes to be donated soon.
- Catalog books, DVDs, and videos.

## Get control of your time

Create a time log. For the next week or two, write down all of the tasks you perform using 15- to 30-minute increments. You may choose to use a basic chart such as the Time Log (Form 8). Use a system that is quick and simple, something you would fill in every day. Keep it visible at all times (e.g., on your desk, in the studio, or in the kitchen).

Fill in all the small things you do outside of the hours you sleep, and may not have noticed before. If you have "perfectionist" tendencies, with an "I will do it myself so it is done right the first time" mentality, consider this: Would you rather have something perfect but delivered late? Clients like reliability. I remember when I first looked at my life pie chart, I was shocked at how many hours I lost on all that was seemingly important.

Do you set aside quality time in your schedule for promotional activities and to look for prospective clients? Plan your time like a drill sergeant with tight and effective time slots. You may have great intentions to accomplish wonderful things, but it takes a great deal of self-discipline to do them efficiently. At the same time, be careful not to become too regimented and lose your spontaneity, sense of creativity, and innovation. Some wonderful things *can* come out of chaos.

The trick is to aim for balance. You need to be determined, have the foresight to carefully strategize over the long term, and implement the most effective system.

# FORM 8
# TIME LOG

| Time | Monday | Tuesday | Wednesday | Thursday | Friday | Saturday | Sunday |
|------|--------|---------|-----------|----------|--------|----------|--------|
| 6:00 a.m. | | | | | | | |
| 6:30 | | | | | | | |
| 7:00 | | | | | | | |
| 7:30 | | | | | | | |
| 8:00 | | | | | | | |
| 8:30 | | | | | | | |
| 9:00 | | | | | | | |
| 9:30 | | | | | | | |
| 10:00 | | | | | | | |
| 10:30 | | | | | | | |
| 11:00 | | | | | | | |
| 11:30 | | | | | | | |
| 12:00 p.m. | | | | | | | |
| 12:30 | | | | | | | |
| 1:00 | | | | | | | |
| 1:30 | | | | | | | |
| 2:00 | | | | | | | |
| 2:30 | | | | | | | |
| 3:00 | | | | | | | |
| 3:30 | | | | | | | |
| 4:00 | | | | | | | |
| 4:30 | | | | | | | |
| 5:00 | | | | | | | |
| 5:30 | | | | | | | |
| 6:00 | | | | | | | |
| 6:30 | | | | | | | |
| 7:00 | | | | | | | |
| 7:30 | | | | | | | |
| 8:00 | | | | | | | |
| 8:30 | | | | | | | |
| 9:00 | | | | | | | |
| 9:30 | | | | | | | |
| 10:00 | | | | | | | |

It's all about self-discipline, especially if you work from home. On your time log include the following nonbusiness activities:

- Sleep
- Grooming
- Getting family prepared and ready for the day
- Preparing breakfast, lunch, and dinner
- Housekeeping
- Grocery shopping
- Fitness
- Socializing
- Entertainment (e.g., watching TV, reading books)

Jot down how long each of the above take in any given day. You'll be surprised at where your time goes.

With those boring but important duties, such as record keeping, filing, and keeping your taxes organized, be aware of spending too much time. When you come to know the flaws in your system and what the ideal system would be, you are halfway toward effective time management. You will find many more hours in your week. I promise!

An eye-opening discovery for me was that it all comes down to habit. Replace your bad habits with good ones, as good habits lead to a more productive and less stressed work life.

Complete Exercise 22 to help you prioritize your time.

# Creating Good Habits

In my former job in the corporate world as a personal assistant I was an organized whiz kid. It was a completely different story, however, when it came to starting and running my own business. At first I was a fire starter, concentrating on activities that brought instant gratification. I enjoyed networking and meeting people and interacting via email and phone. Spurred by enthusiasm and fear of failure, I focused a lot of the time on bringing in clients through marketing and promoting the business.

In the first year I had to learn the importance of daily routine. I originally thought it wasn't going to be a problem locating the necessary documents for my accountant, but I quickly learned my lesson the hard way, spending stressful hours rifling through a box as the tax-filing deadline loomed. From then on I scheduled a regular time (weekly worked for me) for filing and record keeping, so that things wouldn't pile up.

I made the effort to stay up to date with these laborious and not-so-fun administrative duties, which also included stock inventory, compiling forecast projections, and bookkeeping.

## Organizing your files

I like the KISS rule (which can stand for something less rude!): Keep It Simply Structured. This is important when it comes to filing. I am a visual person — I naturally veered toward a color-coordinated filing system.

## EXERCISE 22
# TIME MANAGEMENT

1.  Number the following factors according to the amount of time you allocate to them at present (1 for most time allocated; 10 for least time allocated):

    _____ Business

    _____ Nuclear family (spouse, children, pets)

    _____ Other family (parents, siblings, nieces and nephews)

    _____ Friends and social life

    _____ Networking

    _____ Hobbies

    _____ Market research for business

    _____ Prospecting for more students

    _____ Physical exercise

    _____ Other: _____

2.  Number the following factors according to the amount of time you would like to allocate to them when you achieve the balance that you need (1 for most time allocated; 10 for least time allocated):

    _____ Business

    _____ Nuclear family (spouse, children, pets)

    _____ Other family (parents, siblings, nieces and nephews)

    _____ Friends and social life

    _____ Networking

    _____ Hobbies

    _____ Market research for business

    _____ Prospecting for more students

    _____ Physical exercise

    _____ Other: _____

The business grew so much within a short time that my first filing system became ineffective and cumbersome; in fact, the cabinet was too small for my needs. So, it was time to revamp it.

I created a list of all the possible categories I dealt with on a regular basis. I bought an accordion file with 31 pockets (representing the days of the month) as well as folders in different colors for documents that I would refer to often, or for bills that were due. I placed the bill or invoice in a slot a week before it was due. That gave me enough time to pay it promptly. (And I would place an action note on the bill if I paid it online.)

When I needed to file receipts I divided them into "personal" and "business" and put them in separate manila envelopes with the name of the month and year. I wrote down the purchased item on the receipt (e.g., printer cartridge, acrylic paint, food) to make it easier when I compiled them for a tax return.

Consider where you would typically look to retrieve your documents. It was no use to file an advertisement or article about a specific school or gallery under their name when I was going to refer to it when considering publicity. Instead, it made more sense to have it in a "publicity" folder, accessible when I was ready to write an article or study advertisements.

Lynda Shulman has been a successful art consultant for more than 20 years. Here is her advice on how to keep files organized:

> The key to a good filing system is that it must work for you. Everyone's brain processes information differently, which must be reflected in your system. The labels on your files must reflect the first place that your brain will take you when you are looking for something. For instance, in my case when I think of service providers, I can never remember the name of the supplier but my brain will instantly say "maintenance contracts." I will open my drawer and there will be a file labeled "maintenance contracts." Nine times out of ten I will find what I am looking for in that file. Even if on a rare occasion things get misfiled, having a good system decreases the likelihood of that happening.

See Sample 11 for the filing system I created for Jolly Good Art.

## Action lists

Writing down to-do lists (or "action lists," as I like to call them) on pieces of paper is a bad idea; they invariably get lost or covered with other documents, files, and books. Instead I used a bright red book for all my action lists (including daily, weekly, monthly, and seasonal to-dos), and in the middle of the book I had a section for my long-term goals and a place to jot down any ideas that came to mind. I knew where to go to without searching for various scraps of paper.

I formed a new habit of sitting down every night and writing down my action list for the next day. I would also review items that I put in the weekly, monthly, or seasonal categories and figure out if they should be done that day. By writing down and bringing forward those actions not yet

**Accountant**

**Administration**
- Jolly Good Art Newsletters
- Photos (e.g., students and staff)

**Art Books**
- Reference list of titles
- Book clubs

**Art Supplies**
- Catalogs

**Business Planning**
- Business plan
- Goal setting

**Charities**
- World Wildlife Fund
- Autism

**Communications**
- Contacts
- Correspondence

**Contacts**
- Clients
- Suppliers
- Publicity
- Networking

**Finance**
- Bank
- Credit card bills
- Credit card receipts
- Debts and bills
- Invoices and receipts
- Personal receipts

**Jolly Good Art Programs (current and past)**
- Adult art classes
- Adult registration
- Children's art classes
- Children's registration
- After-school program

**Jolly Good Art Birthday Parties**
- Packages (current and past)

**Jolly Good Art Seasonal Camps**
- March camp
  - March camp registration
- Summer camp
  - Summer camp registration

**Marketing**
- Advertisements
- Publicity
- Leaflets
- Website
- Photos
- Leads (other adverts)
- Miscellaneous lead ideas
- Competition (e.g., art schools, community centers, courses, and galleries)

**Recipes**

**Special Occasion Events**
- Annual Jolly Good Art Exhibition

**Staff**
- Assistants
- Specialist teachers

**Stationery and Furniture Supplies**
- Catalogs
- Business cards
- Contacts

**Utilities**
- Business and cell phone bills
- Car
  - Payments
  - Insurance
- Percentage of home utilities used for business

completed, I cleared my mind instead of leaving them going around in my head in the "twilight zone" of falling asleep.

Then I would look at the action list the next morning, either in the kitchen or at my desk. Sitting down with my red book gave my days and weeks much-needed structure. It gave me a sense of control and confidence. Maintain this good habit and ignore the disruptions.

Sample 12 is an action list as it may typically look on a Sunday evening or Monday morning. Here, a lot of the weekly tasks get transferred to the top of the list.

## Calendars and program plans

I did not want to spare the time to learn how to use a portable, palm-held computer — I preferred to spend the time and money on a digital camera and upgrading my scanner and computer so I could upload students' artwork onto my website.

I depended on a large desk calendar, putting start and end dates of all of my classes. Later on I learned to use and depend on the electronic calendar in Microsoft Works. The couple of hours it took me to learn it was worth it for one major reason: it flashed reminders on the computer screen at the date and time of an appointment or a task I had planned.

For each class, camp, and special occasion such as a party and charity event, I would create a simple spreadsheet. Along with all the dates and times I'd list all the projects I'd be giving them (sometimes summer camps had three or four projects in a week), all the students' names, and what snacks or lunch I would be serving.

Every morning the calendar, along with my red action book, ensured that I was absolutely up to date, and that I wouldn't miss any business opportunities. (It also ensured that I wouldn't incur any library fines!)

I also kept a small calendar in my handbag. I made a daily habit of transferring any appointments or details onto the computer database to keep it all synchronized.

Remember to keep all your time planning devices up to date. The system is only as good as your input. Make it part of your daily routine.

## Electronic management

There are many options available for managing a database of information, including your schedule, electronically. The program Microsoft Outlook is not only an email program; it also features a calendar and can manage your contacts. And despite what I said, do consider PDAs — personal digital assistants — to make all this information portable. (Go to www.palm.com and www.blackberry.com to check out the latest models.) Research on the Internet and ask around what systems people use and what they like and do not like about them.

I myself used a simple electronic database with the details of all my students (e.g., name of guardian, age, address, and when and what program taken or inquired about), as well as all my other contacts including suppliers and professional friends. Whenever there was something I wanted all of these people to know about, I printed a list of their names and phoned them over a few days, or I mailed out customized newsletters, with which I sometimes included vouchers or copies of news article clippings.

# A TYPICAL ACTION LIST

**To-do today**
- Phone (or return calls to) prospective and current clients, including those requesting a birthday party event
- Make weekly menu and shopping list for home, in-class snacks, and birthday party event(s)
- Prepare lesson plans and curriculum for birthday party event(s)
- Sort incoming mail
- Return email
- File documents and receipts

**Weekly**
- Review business plan, including marketing plan
- Do housekeeping
- Go grocery shopping
- Deposit checks

**Biweekly**
- Compile a newsletter
- Reconnect with friends and contacts in network; arrange lunch meeting

**Monthly**
- Review "big picture" action plan, and figure out what is and is not working
- Think about writing an article, or what newsworthy activities could be included in a press release
- Update website (e.g., news, artwork, accolades, awards)
- Schedule family time (e.g., one Sunday a month free from business)

**Seasonal**
- Plan seasonal camps and special occasion events such as an annual art exhibition or crafts for a charity
- Plan lunch menu for these camps and events

# Prioritize Work and Play

No matter how well you plan to keep your personal and business lives separate and healthy, life in general, and especially the drive to succeed, can interfere or even take over.

In the first year it wasn't really an option to outsource jobs to anyone else (e.g., web design, bookkeeping) or to hire staff or specialist teachers. I had to learn to depend on myself. This included trusting my own judgment; prioritizing, organizing, and delegating in business and at home; setting a less rigorous pace for myself; and lessening stress by taking time out for myself.

Study the way you handle stress, including the stress of multitasking. The suggestions in this chapter should help you, as well as advice from those around you.

One of the most difficult things for entrepreneurs while they juggle home-based businesses with family is to achieve *balance*. You will sometimes find it impossible to close the office or studio door at the end of the working day and turn off the stress. Even if you do not have too many family commitments, or you are superorganized, you still need to prioritize areas of your life outside of work. Leave enough time and energy to socialize and relax. You can easily turn into a workaholic if you do not respect the health of your mind and body. Watch out for the risks and signs of burnout, as discussed later in this chapter.

I made a pact with myself early on to forfeit some things in order to make better use of my time. I decided that I could live without the long lunches I used to have every two weeks with friends, the hours of watching TV and movies (with or without my ten-year-old daughter), and the personal shopping.

What I refused to give up were dates with my husband, lunches with my daughter, reading, creating art, writing, and a movie once a week. I found that if I worked through seven days of the week without my "romantic date with husband" or "movie fix," the stress would inevitably catch up with me. It would sap my energy, and my creativity and productivity levels would suffer.

I was also unwilling to sacrifice my reading habits. I read anything to do with business, motivational how-to books, and inspiring art books and magazines, but this was all work related. For relaxation, I read a myriad of fiction. As the business grew, time became increasingly limited, and relaxation was crucial. Reading fiction before going to sleep gave me the escape I craved, serving as a buffer between my working hours and my rest. If I did not remove myself mentally and physically from the computer and the art studio and went straight to sleep without a half-hour fiction read, my brain continued whirling around the dozens of things still left to do, and invariably I woke up tired and not refreshed.

Find out what recharges and revitalizes your spiritual and mental well-being. At least a 20- to 30-minute walk a day, or any other fitness regime of your choice will give your whole body, mind, and spirit a boost. Invest in this time and your productivity and quality of life will increase tremendously.

Consider what you are willing and not willing to sacrifice when it comes to how you spend your time. There is nothing wrong with being driven or ambitious — you must be to a certain extent in order to succeed; however, you must achieve a balance. I believe it is possible, since I have done so myself.

## Schedule leisure time

We all need a day or week to regroup, re-energize, and reconnect with ourselves and our loved ones. But be warned: even on a relaxing day trip with my cell phone turned off and a rule to not even mention the business, I had to consciously click off from "work" mode. It was very difficult in the first two years. Sometimes it took me the entire day to start to unwind. It was difficult to stop the whirl of my business brain, which was interfering with my off time. I eventually learned that letting go and relaxing as quickly as possible meant more quality time with my family and more time to revitalize. It is all about the mind-set and the messages we send to ourselves.

Make time for the following:

- Friends and family
- Holidays
- Fitness
- Hobbies

Now I know I considered some of these as "time thieves" earlier in this chapter, but it is all about organizing your priorities, which includes setting aside time for recharging. For example, I love experimenting, creating art or painting without any expectations of a finished product to show for my time and energy.

What about learning to play a musical instrument, or woodworking, or something completely different from what you usually do? My friend Traci Tomkin regularly welcomes people from the corporate world to her "Throwing a Fit" sessions so they can de-stress by creating with clay. Hours of play keep the stress monster at bay. Really!

You must schedule a specific amount of leisure time into your calendar, or your business will steal all your physical and psychological resources, that is, your enthusiasm, motivation, and energy. The sense of self-achievement and self-esteem can suffer from being pushed and pulled in so many directions. It is easy to become immune to the wonders of your life and lose your sense of priority or direction. Take a step back and make sure that you are not being controlled by your business, and instead that it's the other way around.

## Schedule family time

We sometimes forget what is important to others since we are blinkered with our own needs and ambitions. How do you cater to your family's needs when the phone rings and business beckons? After all, most parents will be calling you in their time off, in the evenings and on weekends. Your family and other loved ones may not be supportive or understanding, especially if you are putting business ahead of them for the first time.

Hold regular family meetings — every two weeks worked for me. Ask for their suggestions and write them down so you can remember key points and validate your commitment. Perhaps they can help you with your business if you give them some incentive?

Do not forget your spouse (if you have one). He or she will support you in many ways, but you must not forget about them, and also your needs as a couple. For example, you may vote to hire a cleaner to give you more time to spend together. It's possible your relationship suffers because of your business success. Beware of self-sabotage in these cases. Discuss any issues as soon as possible. If you recognize problems early enough you can try and rectify them before they have had a chance to become ingrained.

Watch out for signs of discord in the family unit such as passive-aggressive behavior. And if your spouse is frustrated or dissatisfied, a child will pick up on that. Children are extremely astute at mimicry. Discuss their concerns and listen to their points of view. Everyone needs validation that they are heard and loved. Communicate what each of your needs are and how you can work together.

One of the ways to make sure you are giving your family enough of your time is by creating time slots in your calendar on a daily or weekly basis. It may take time to make this a part of the family routine, but the quality and content of your time together will have much more meaning than if you are feeling pressured, rushed, or guilt-tripped into it.

Together make a list and plan for what you can do as a family. Respect this time as sacred. Make a conscious effort to keep promises, such as not answering the business phone or popping into the office for any reason.

Close the office and studio doors during this time. If you are like me, the break from the business and reconnection with family will invigorate you. When you go back to your business tasks, you will feel proud of having looked after your family's needs. You will have struck the balance that comes with running a successful business *and* being part of a happy family.

If art, teaching, and business are your passions, you may find that the hours fly by and your personal life and work life become too difficult to separate. Take control of your time, get organized, stay focused on your goals, and ask your network of friends and family to help you strike a healthy balance between your work and your life.

# Risks and Signs of Burnout

The risk of burnout exists in many occupations, and you may get drawn into it if you do not know any other way of achieving and maintaining success. The following are some symptoms:

- Your brain is forever juggling dozens of things you need to do (e.g., having to follow up on leads, order and buy more art supplies, create snacks for classes).

- You do too much in a day and you want to do more, moving more and more items on the to-do list for the next day (e.g., phoning a list of clients you did not get around to earlier).

- You become forgetful and lose documents or lists (e.g., tax documents for your accountant are not all together in one file; you run out of stock, forgetting to keep the inventory list up to date).

- You feel increasingly overwhelmed by business and family life, unable to keep up with everyday demands (e.g., you cannot go on your child's school trips and consequently feel guilty).

- You become irritable.

- You make pains to hide your tiredness from your clients or your family.

- You delay or forfeit holidays due to the fear of missing important business and having to return to a backlog.

- You experience pain in the chest that does not go away even when you are away on vacation, as well as headaches and other ailments stemming from stress, anxiety, or tension.

- You constantly think or talk about business.

- Sometimes you feel teary and find it hard to stay positive every day, such as when you interact with children, students, and staff.

- You go to sleep later each night, and you sometimes have to pull yourself out of bed because you do not have the drive and joy you had before.

Even if you recognize yourself in only a few of the above examples and you really do not think you have an issue right now, just keep these symptoms in mind so that you do not burn out in the future.

You should also consider doing positive "mind and spirit" activities such as meditation, yoga, and dance. These can really revitalize the whole you.

If you find you don't have enough time to do everything you want to, rework your schedule. Perhaps your friends and loved ones can help you out. Don't forget how important it is to *delegate* — you have the best resources and you can afford to do so. Learn to trust yourself and others, and identify any problems before they become major.

# GROWING YOUR BUSINESS

*The future you see is the future you get.*

— ROBERT G. ALLEN

This chapter will give you ideas on how you can prepare for diversification and growth of the business in your own unique way. Remember, you are creating a niche market for your business and keeping it exciting, fresh, and profitable, so you will stay motivated doing what you love.

## Branching into the Next Phase of Your Business

A year or two after your successful start you may be ready to consider growing your business. Now you have the advantage of actually having lived and done it rather than theorizing, second-guessing, dreaming, and hoping. You will have learned the many hard truths and intricacies of starting

and running a business. You must now consider the following questions regarding your business's growth:

- Are you capable of branching out?

- Do you feel ready?

- How far and how fast would you like to expand?

## Organize artist's retreats

After months or years of getting to know your students and their families, you may want to organize artist's retreats for small groups. These can take place for a week or a weekend in the summer at an idyllic cottage with lush gardens that would inspire even the most tired, jaded, or creatively blocked.

You must think about transportation, the facilities, the food, and what materials to bring, and if guests will be sharing accommodation or prefer private quarters. You also have to take into account how much time this will take for you and your staff.

You will have the opportunity to craft unique packages. Your ongoing market research and surveys will help you keep up with what the customer wants.

If taking children on these trips, make sure you have a waiver or permission form that will give you as much information as possible. You can use the Release Form for Field Trips (Form 1) from Chapter 3 and rework it for an artist's retreat.

## Create additional programs

Consider offering your services elsewhere. For example, you could offer your programs to schools for children with special needs or at residential homes for seniors. These clients will be just as eager to be creative and learn new art media. Create programs that can be easily executed by you and your staff outside of the studio.

Keep your projects audience-appropriate. Ask for feedback after the sessions. How well was the class received and how could it be improved? What was missing? Were there any parts that were too long?

You may be able to get commitment to more classes — the students might be fired up and raring to go the next level. Be prepared and bring registration forms, and offer instant registration discounts.

Providing the best possible experience to everyone will lead to word-of-mouth recommendations, which are the best compliment and the strongest way to grow.

## Sell art supplies

Demand leads to supply, especially if you are going through huge amounts of art materials for your school and for students to use outside of class. (Create a simple inventory system so you do not run out of stock.) Try to get bulk discounts for the items that you go through quickly, and think about selling them (at a small profit) to your students — for example, small and large canvases, watercolor and acrylic paints, and oil and chalk pastel packs. Other items you can sell are paintbrushes, latex gloves, charcoal sticks, pencils, and sketch and other pads.

Another possibility is to create special gift baskets or packages, which students or parents can buy for their children or friends. Use items from your bulk stock to assemble these.

Consider buying some art supplies from wholesale suppliers, even directly from Asian importers. It never hurts to do your homework, especially if it works out to be very economically viable. Learning the ropes of buying and selling may be worth your time, and the profits may be exciting enough to diversify into this lucrative outlet. Make sure you have researched all the tax and other legal requirements and restrictions as discussed in Chapter 1.

## Collaborate

I enjoy collaboration, whether it's on a temporary or permanent basis. Consider sharing a larger space where there is a gallery, even if it's just a makeshift space that showcases art such as pottery, silk painting, and multimedia quilts.

If your studio is large enough to set up a spacious, well-lit gallery, you can utilize your own and your students' — as well as your collaborators' — art pieces.

You could also partner up with a picture-framing business and have a dedicated wall of frame samples and paintings to show the available service by this other business. As we have discussed in the chapter on networking, there are many options, as long as you go into partnerships well informed.

## Franchise

Another way to branch out is by franchising, either buying into a franchise or selling your business as a franchise. Although this book concentrates on a start-up enterprise, you may want to do some research on this.

There are many books and websites, especially the US and Canadian government sites mentioned in the resources section on the CD-ROM, that are dedicated to the many opportunities for art-related businesses. If you are franchising, think about your business as your baby that has grown over time. You want to make sure that whoever uses your company's name will keep to the high standards that you have created and that your clients expect.

If you are buying into someone else's franchise, you may or may not be able to take on their customers, as your way of teaching may or may not align with the previous owner's reputation. Be aware that it may cost much more to go this route than if you were to start on your own from scratch.

## How Fast Should You Expand Your Business?

Some people are driven to succeed even more, even if it appears that they have "made it." I believe in the adage "success breeds success," and that expansion will become a natural route to take. However, beware of becoming greedy or impatient about growing your business without proper thought and planning.

When you grow at a steady pace and form a solid foundation, you are more likely to be in control of where your enterprise is heading. However, if you go to the next level without considering the risks, you may lose the reins and become overwhelmed.

The following is an example of what can happen if you expand too rapidly.

Tina was riding high, excited by her growing business. She jumped at the chance to rent a studio double the size of her home-based studio. For one thing, she was excited about the new location, which was next to restaurants and a popular clothing store in a busy plaza. "Mothers, children, and prospective clients everywhere," she thought gleefully. In her new location people passing by could come in and ask about her services at any time during open hours. Obviously, this was not the case with her home-based studio.

Unfortunately, she had not considered the following necessities:

- A lease contract with a minimum of two years

- Increased rental fees and bills
- The necessity of more classes and programs, and/or a price increase, in order to cover initial costs (e.g., redecorating and deposit fees)
- The necessity of more staff because of the additional programs

At her new premises she was under immense pressure to "make it pay." She had not accounted for the complications and costs of day care, or the high heating and air-conditioning bills throughout the year. In her home studio she could claim tax benefits such as a portion of her bills. And she was spending less time with her family because of the after-school and evening classes she now had to add to her business curriculum. It was taking all the passion out of her love of teaching, and she felt the business was controlling her instead of the other way around.

The straw that broke this entrepreneur's back was having to walk alone to her car in a secluded parking lot late at night, after the classes were finally over.

---

I am not trying to draw a dark picture or dissuade you from the idea of expanding to the next level. Just make sure you consider everything and work through all the practical issues that may arise. You need to create a contingency plan.

Even successful businesses take time to grow. Think about the empty nester who opens up a yoga instruction studio. She diligently grows her clientele over a period of one or two years, and within three years she builds a successful studio with many excellent, reliable staff to whom she delegates the teaching responsibilities.

Create a SCOT analysis of the pros and cons of growing or branching out into a different area, and then get started with your new venture!

If you are the type of person who does not like to stay in certain situations for too long, afraid of boredom or of your services becoming stale, but also of making a wrong decision, then schedule some time to revisit creative visualization and goal-setting exercises and delve deeper into your original visions for your life and business. Talk it over with your mentor, friends, and those near and dear to you. Calculate any risks and changes, but be true to your own heart and your own instincts.

If you have truly considered all the steps throughout this book, then this is what you will have achieved:

- A better understanding of yourself and others
- Conceptualization of your business and market research
- Your own unique programs
- Knowledge of how to build a wonderful support system
- The skills to inspire and communicate through your promotional literature, including your website
- Confidence in your organizational skills

You've established a taste for business, a growing client base, and momentum, and you are ready to grow to the next level. You'll have the opportunity to share your love of art and teaching with a larger group of clients.

This is the next phase of your journey of discovery — now go for it. Let your innovation and creativity flourish. Inner confidence will keep you cool and serene as you embark on the roller-coaster ride that is your business.

Jolly Good Luck!

# Appendix
## SELECTED BIBLIOGRAPHY

## Chapter 1:
## Getting Your Business Started

Beare, Helen. *How to Avoid Business Failure.* Sheldon Press, 1993.

De Young, John Edward. *Cases in Small Business Management: A Strategic Problems Approach.* Upstart Pub. Co., 3rd edition, 1994.

Duoba, John L., ed. *Launching Your First Small Business: Make the Right Decisions During Your First 90 Days.* CCH Business, 2nd edition, 2003.

Karlson, David. *Avoiding Mistakes in Your Small Business: Profiting from the Experiences of Others.* Crisp Publications, 1994.

Longsworth, Elizabeth K. *Anatomy of a Start-up: Why Some New Businesses Succeed and Others Fail.* Inc. Publishing, 1991.

McGuckin, Frances. *Big Ideas for Growing Your Small Business: How to Build Profits and Manage Growth.* Eastleigh Publications, 2nd edition, 2004.

_____. *Business for Beginners: From Research and Business Plans to Money, Marketing, and the Law.* Sourcebooks Inc., US edition, 2005.

Pinson, Linda, and Jerry Jinnett. *The Home-Based Entrepreneur.* Upstart Pub. Co., 2nd edition, 1993.

Podmoroff, Diana. *How to Hire, Train & Keep the Best Employees for Your Small Business.* Atlantic Publishing Company, 2004.

Portman, Janet, and Fred S. Steingold. *Negotiate the Best Lease for Your Business*. Nolo, 2nd edition, 2005.

Robertson, Heather, ed. *Taking Care of Business: Stories of Canadian Women Entrepreneurs*. Fenn, 1997.

Sitarz, Daniel. *The Complete Book of Small Business Management Forms*. Nova, 2001.

Wolter, Romanus. *Kick Start Your Dream Business: Getting It Started and Keeping You Going*. Ten Speed Press, 2001.

## Chapter 2: Becoming a Multifaceted Entrepreneur

Berens, Linda V. *Understanding Yourself and Others: An Introduction to the 4 Temperaments*. Telos Publications, 2006.

Carnegie, Dale. *How to Stop Worrying and Start Living*. Pocket Books, rev. edition, 2004.

_____. *How To Win Friends & Influence People*. Vermilion, new edition, 2007.

_____. *The Quick and Easy Way to Effective Speaking*. Pentagon Press, 2006.

De Bono, Edward. *I Am Right, You Are Wrong: From This to the New Renaissance: From Rock Logic to Water Logic*. Penguin Books, 1992.

_____. *Six Thinking Hats*. Penguin Books, 2nd edition, 2000.

Friedman, Meyer, and Diane Ulmer. *Treating Type A Behavior — and Your Heart*. Alfred A. Knopf, 1987.

Gardner, Howard. *The Unschooled Mind: How Children Think and How Schools Should Teach*. Basic Books, reissue edition, 1993.

Pell, Arthur R. *Enrich Your Life the Dale Carnegie Way*. Dale Carnegie & Assoc., 1979.

Tieger, Paul D., and Barbara Barron-Tieger. *Do What You Are: Discover the Perfect Career for You Through the Secrets of Personality Type*. Little Brown & Co., 1992.

## Chapter 3: Organizing Your Classes

Most of these are from my personal collection of books on parenting, psychology, and teaching. I have found them to be incredibly beneficial in many ways. Some may be "classics" but you may search on the Internet and your library for similar or more specific resources that suit your own needs for inspiration or for more information.

### Psychological, Teaching, and Learning Guides

De Bono, Edward. *Practical Thinking: 4 Ways to Be Right, 5 Ways to Be Wrong, 5 Ways to Understand*. Penguin USA, 1992.

_____. *Serious Creativity: Using the Power of Lateral Thinking to Create New Ideas*. HarperBusiness, 1993.

_____. *Teach Your Child How to Think*. Penguin Books, 1994.

Erikson, Erik. *Childhood and Society*. Triad, 1981.

Gordon, Thomas. *P.E.T.: Parent Effectiveness Training: The Proven Program for Raising Responsible Children*. Three Rivers Press, rev. edition, 2000.

Holt, John. *How Children Fail*. Perseus Pub., rev. edition, 1995.

Hopkins, Lee Bennett. *Let Them Be Themselves*. HarperCollins Children's Books, 3rd edition, 1992.

Kuczen, Barbara. *Childhood Stress*. Delta Books, 1987.

Mosston, Muska. *Teaching: From Command to Discovery*. Wadsworth Pub. Co., 1998.

Smutny, Joan Franklin. *Your Gifted Child: How to Recognize and Develop the Special Talents in Your Child from Birth to Age Seven*. Ballantine, 1989.

Stant, Margaret A. *The Young Child: His Activities and Materials*. Prentice Hall, 1972. (Although this is more about the preschooler, it is a worthwhile classic.)

Winnicott, D. W. *Home Is Where We Start From*. Penguin, 1990.

Wright, H. Norman. *The Power of a Parent's Words: How You Can Use Loving, Effective Communication to Increase Your Child's Self-esteem and Reduce the Frustrations of Parenting*. Regal Books, 1991.

### Children with Special Needs

Dillon, Kathleen M. *Living with Autism: The Parents' Stories*. Parkway Publishers, 1995.

# Chapter 4:
# Class Prices and Materials

### Art Books

Try to get a hold of art books on the Classic and Impressionist masters. Some of my personal favorites are Raphael, Manet, Klimt, Rubens, da Vinci, Rembrandt, Van Gogh, Kandinsky, Renoir, Chagall, Monet, Modigliani, Cezanne, Degas, and Gauguin.

Also look for any books by or about wildlife painter Robert Bateman.

Cheshire, Jane, and Rowena Stott. *The Country Diary Book of Stencilling*. Bloomsbury Books, 1988.

Meehan, Patricia, and Les Meehan. *The Creative Stencil Source Book: 200 Inspiring and Original Motifs*. Sterling, 2000.

Singer, Alan. *Wildlife Art*. Rockport Publishers, 1999.

Taylor, Denise Westcott. *Seashore Designs*. Merehurst, 1999.

Wellford, Lin. *The Art of Painting Animals on Rocks*. North Light Books, 1999.

_____. *Painting Pets on Rocks*. North Light Books, 2000.

### Craft, Beads, Mosaics, etc.

Beesley, Terrece, and Trice Boerens. *Fabric Mosaics*. That Patchwork Place, 1999.

Biggs, Emma, and Tessa Hunkin. *Outdoor Mosaic: Original Weather Proof Designs to Brighten Any Exterior Space*. Trafalgar Square Publishing, 2001.

Donnelly, Sarah. *Easy Mosaics for Your Home and Garden*. North Light Books, 2001.

Duncan Aimone, Katherine. *The Beaded Home: Simply Beautiful Projects*. Lark Books, 2002.

Graivier Bell, Tracy, and Sarah Kelly. *Crazy Mosaic*. Laurel Glen Publishing, 2002.

Van Wagner Childs, Anne. *Creative Touches: How to Add Flair to Ready-to-Wear*. Leisure Arts, 1992.

## Glass Painting

Dunsterville, Jane. *The Glass Painting Book.* David & Charles, 2003.

_____, and John Dunsterville. *Glass Painting Projects: Decorative Glass for Beautiful Interiors.* David & Charles, 2001.

Neal, Moira, and Lynda Howarth. *Painting Glass in a Weekend.* New Holland Publishers, 2002.

## Silk Painting

Hahn, Susanne. *A Complete Guide to Silk Painting.* Search Press, 1995.

Kennedy, Jill, and Jane Varrall. *Silk Painting: New Ideas and Textures.* Dover, 1994.

Southan, Mandy. *Beginner's Guide to Silk Painting.* Search Press, 1997.

Zhen, Lian Quan. *Chinese Painting Techniques for Exquisite Watercolors.* North Light Books, 2004.

## Technique

Bays, Jill. *Flowers in the Landscape.* David & Charles, 2003.

Buckley, Sarah. *Practical Watercolour Techniques.* Crescent, 1992.

Crabb, Thomas. *A Beginner's Guide to Painting & Drawing.* Bounty Books, 1991.

Crawshaw, Alwyn. *The Half-Hour Painter: Paint a Successful Landscape in 30 Minutes.* Collins, new edition, 1997.

Edward, Betty. *The New Drawing on the Right Side of the Brain.* HarperCollins, revised edition, 2001.

_____. *The New Drawing on the Right Side of the Brain Workbook: Guided Practice in the Five Basic Skills of Drawing.* Penguin Putnam, 2002.

Fotherby, Lesley. *Cats: Drawing & Painting in Watercolour.* Trans-Atlantic Publications, 1999.

Gair, Angela. *The Drawing and Painting Course.* Bookmart, 1997.

Hammond, Lee. *How to Draw Lifelike Portraits from Photographs.* North Light Books, 1995.

Howard, Ken, ed. *Art Class: A Beginner's Complete Guide to Painting and Drawing.* Quadrillion Media, 1999.

Kunz, Jan. *Painting Watercolour Florals that Glow.* Cassell Illustrated, 1995.

Parramón's Editorial Team. *Painting Landscapes in Watercolors.* Barron's Educational Series, 1996.

Rubin Wolf, Rachel, ed. *Basic Flower Painting Techniques in Watercolor: Techniques in Watercolor.* North Light Books, 1996.

_____, ed. *Keys to Painting Fur & Feathers.* North Light Books, 1999.

Seslar, Patrick. *The One-Hour Watercolorist.* North Light Books, 2001.

Soan, Hazel. *Vibrant Watercolours.* Collins, 2005.

Whittlesea, Michael. *The Complete Step-by-Step Watercolour Course.* Chancellor Press, 1992.

## Pastels

Constance, Diana. *Pastels: Ron Ranson's Painting School.* Pub Overstock Unlimited Inc., 1995.

Harrison, Hazel. *Pastels: Art School Pastels: Step-By-Step Teaching Through Inspirational Projects.* Lorenz Books, 1998.

Parramón, Jose Maria. *Painting Landscapes & Figures in Pastel*. Watson-Guptill Publications, 1990.

Rodden, Guy. *Pastel Painting Techniques: 17 Pastel Projects, Illustrated Step-by-Step with Advice on Materials and Techniques*. Cassell Illustrated, 1991.

## Chapter 5: Your Business Plan

Covello, Joseph, and Brian Hazelgren. *Your First Business Plan: A Simple Question-and-Answer Format Designed to Help You Write Your Own Plan*. Sourcebooks, 5th edition, 2005.

Henricks, Mark. *Business Plans Made Easy: It's Not as Hard as You Think*. Entrepreneur Media Inc., 2nd edition, 2002.

Magos, Alice H. *Business Plans That Work for Your Small Business*. CCH Inc., 2nd edition, 2003.

Mohr, Angie. *Bookkeepers' Boot Camp: Get a Grip on Accounting Basics*. Self-Counsel Press, 2003.

_____. *Financial Management 101: Get a Grip on Your Business Numbers*. Self-Counsel Press, 2003.

Patsula, Peter J. *Successful Business Planning in 30 Days: A Step-By-Step Guide For Writing a Business Plan and Starting Your Own Business*. Prentice Hall, 2004.

Pinson, Linda. *Keeping the Books: Basic Record Keeping and Accounting for the Successful Business*. Kaplan Business, 6th edition, 2004.

## Chapter 6: Identifying and Targeting Your Market

Doman, Don, Dell Dennison, and Margaret Doman. *Market Research Made Easy*. Self-Counsel Press, 3rd edition, 2006.

Fletcher, Tana, and Julia Rockler. *Getting Publicity*. Self-Counsel Press, 3rd edition, 2000.

Goldman, Heinz M. *How to Win Customers*. Pan Macmillan, 1993.

Goldstein, Leslie S. *Finding New Customers for Your Business*. VHS. American Business Video Training Series. American Business Videos [distributor].

Harvard Business Review and Harvard Business School Press. *How to Price Your Product*. McGraw-Hill Companies, 1991.

Kahle, Dave J. *The Six-Hat Salesperson: A Dynamic Approach to Producing Top Results in Every Selling Situation*. AMACOM/ American Management Services, 1999.

Kotler, Philip. *Kotler on Marketing: How to Create, Win, and Dominate Markets*. Free Press, 1999.

Pinson, Linda, and Jerry Jinnett. *Target Marketing: Researching, Reaching and Retaining Your Target Market*. Upstart Pub. Co., 3rd edition, 1996.

Roffer, Robin Fisher. *Make a Name for Yourself: Eight Steps Every Woman Needs to Create a Personal Brand Strategy for Success*. Broadway Books, 2002.

Thomas, Bob. *The Fail-proof Enterprise: A Success Model for Entrepreneurs*. Hillsdale College Press, 1999.

Vogelaar, Donald. *Know Your Customer: Using Practical Market Research for Profit.* Prentice Hall, 1992.

Withers, Jean, and Carol Vipperman. *Marketing Your Service.* Self-Counsel Press, 3rd edition, 1998.

## Chapter 7: Creating Your Web Presence

Berkley, Holly. *Low-Budget Online Marketing.* Self-Counsel Press, 2nd edition, 2005.

Gregory, Kip. *Winning Clients in a Wired World: Seven Strategies for Growing Your Business Using Technology and the Web.* John Wiley & Sons Inc., 2004.

MacDonald, Matthew. *Creating Web Sites: The Missing Manual.* O'Reilly Media, 2006.

Musciano, Chuck, and Bill Kennedy. *HTML and XHTML: The Definitive Guide.* O'Reilly Media, 2006.

Robbins, Jennifer Niederst. *Learning Web Design: A Beginner's Guide to HTML, Graphics, and Beyond.* O'Reilly Media, 3rd edition, 2007.

_____. *Web Design in a Nutshell: A Desktop Quick Reference.* O'Reilly Media, 3rd edition, 2006.

Smith, Bud E., and Arthur Bebak. *Creating Web Pages for Dummies.* Wiley, 8th edition, 2007.

## Chapter 8: Interviewing and Hiring Employees

*Employee Management Forms Kit.* CD-ROM. Self-Counsel Press, 2007.

Grensing-Pophal, Lin. *Employee Management for Small Business.* Self-Counsel Press, 2nd edition, 2005.

Mornell, Pierre. *45 Effective Ways for Hiring Smart: How to Predict Winners and Losers in the Incredibly Expensive People-Reading Game.* Ten Speed Press, 2003.

## Chapter 9: Networking

Also see titles by Dale Carnegie as recommended in the bibliography for Chapter 1, above.

Covey, Stephen R. *The 7 Habits of Highly Effective People.* Simon & Schuster, 2005.

## Chapter 10: Get Organized and Stay Organized

Aslett, Don. *Clutter's Last Stand: It's Time to De-junk Your Life!* Adams Media Corporation, 2nd edition, 2005.

Blanchard, Kenneth, and Robert Lorber. *Putting the One Minute Manager to Work: How to Turn the 3 Secrets into Skills.* William Morrow, 2006.

Covey, Stephen R. *The 7 Habits of Highly Effective People.* Simon & Schuster, 2005.

Francis, Linda Leigh. *Run Your Business So It Doesn't Run You.* Borah Press, 2003.

Haneberg, Lisa. *Coaching Basics.* ASTD Press, 2006.

_____. *Focus Like a Laser Beam: 10 Ways to Do What Matters Most.* Jossey-Bass, 2006.

Hemphill, Barbara. *Taming the Paper Tiger at Home.* Kaplan Business, 6th edition, 2005.

_____. *Taming the Paper Tiger at Work.* Kaplan Business, 3rd edition, 2005.

Koch, Richard. *Living the 80/20 Way: Work Less, Worry Less, Succeed More, Enjoy More.* Nicholas Brealey Pub., 2005.

Lakein, Alan. *How to Get Control of Your Time and Your Life*. Signet, 1989.

Lively, Lynn. *The Procrastinator's Guide to Success*. McGraw-Hill, 1999.

Meyer, Jeffrey J. *Time Management for Dummies*. For Dummies, 2nd edition, 1999.

Morgenstern, Julie. *Organizing from the Inside Out: The Foolproof System for Organizing Your Home, Your Office, and Your Life*. Henry Holt and Company, 2nd edition, 2004.

Williams, Debbie. *Home Management 101: A Guide for Busy Parents*. Champion Press, 2001.

## Chapter 11:
## Growing Your Business

Fritz, Roger. *The Small Business Troubleshooter: 152 Solutions to the Problems Faced by Every Growing Company*. Unlimited Publishing, 2nd edition, 2000.

Gerber, Michael E. *The E-Myth Revisited: Why Most Small Businesses Don't Work and What to Do About It*. Collins, rev. edition, 2005.

Griffiths, Andrew. *101 Survival Tips for Your Business: Practical Tips to Help Your Business Survive and Prosper*. Allen and Unwin, 2002.

Judson, Bruce. *Go It Alone!: The Secret to Building a Successful Business on Your Own*. Collins, 2005.

Karlson, David. *Avoiding Mistakes in Your Small Business: Profiting from the Experiences of Others*. Crisp Learning, 1994.

Lonier, Terri. *The Frugal Entrepreneur: Creative Ways to Save Time, Energy, & Money in Your Business*. Portico Press, 1996.

## Personal Development and Other Inspirational Books

Bendaly, Leslie. *Winner Instinct: The 6 New Laws of Success*. HarperCollins, 2000.

Cameron, Julia. *The Artist's Way: A Spiritual Path to Higher Creativity*. Tarcher/Putnam, 2002.

_____. *The Vein of Gold: A Journey to Your Creative Heart*. Tarcher/Putnam, 1996.

Carnegie, Dale. *How to Stop Worrying and Start Living*. Pocket Books, rev. edition, 2004.

Covey, Stephen R. *The 7 Habits of Highly Effective People*. Simon & Schuster, 2005.

Jeffers, Susan. *Feel the Fear ... and Do It Anyway*. Ballantine Books, 2006.

Morgenstern, Julie. *Organizing from the Inside Out: The Foolproof System for Organizing Your Home, Your Office, and Your Life*. Henry Holt and Company, 2nd edition, 2004.

Richardson, Cheryl. *Stand Up for Your Life: Develop the Courage, Confidence, and Character to Fulfill Your Greatest Potential*. Bantam, 2003.

# OTHER TITLES FROM SELF-COUNSEL PRESS

## Start & Run a Creative Services Business

Susan Kirkland
ISBN 13: 978-1-55180-607-5 • ISBN 10: 1-55180-607-X
$17.95 US / $22.95 Cdn

This book shows how creative professionals such as free-lance graphic designers, writers, illustrators, and photographers can run successful businesses without leaving their computers. With the tips and first-person accounts in this book, you can run a successful business working for yourself and doing creative work you enjoy.

Create an electronic portfolio, target your market on-line, and distinguish yourself from the competition. Susan Kirkland shares tips and techniques to overcome self-doubt, find and keep clients, buy the right equipment, team up with professional peers, and make more money.

## Start & Run a Gift Basket Business

Mardi Foster-Walker
ISBN 13: 978-1-55180-503-0 • ISBN 10: 1-55180-503-0
$17.95 US / $22.95 Cdn

With little more than some working space and a few basket-making items, an ambitious and creative person can cash in on the gift basket boom. The potential for unearthing new markets and finding motivated clients is unlimited in this easy-to-run small business.

Topics include:

- Researching the existing market
- Finding a suitable work space
- Pricing the gift baskets
- Creating theme and seasonal baskets
- Dealing with wholesalers
- Finding clients
- Advertising and promoting your service

The following are included on the enclosed CD-ROM for use on a Windows-based PC. The forms and exercises are in PDF and MS Word formats.

**Forms**

- Release form for field trips
- Registration form
- Summer camp confirmation
- Seasonal camp survey
- Birthday party planning
- Projected income and operating costs
- Personal cash flow statement
- Interview questions
- Time log

**Exercises**

- Creative visualization
- Setting your goals
- Conceptualizing your art-related business
- Are you ready to begin?
- Where will you start your business?
- Choosing your business name
- Are you an entrepreneur?
- Personality strengths and challenges
- Shyness and assertiveness
- Learning styles
- Do you have what it takes?

- Researching your competition
- Seasonal programs
- Visualize your action plan
- Targeting your market
- Know your clients
- Your competitors
- Researching and writing articles
- Preparing for a website
- Finding a networking group
- Should you hire a coach or mentor?
- Time management

**Sample marketing material from Jolly Good Art, including flyers and newsletters**

**Sample invoice/agreement**

**Recipe for Yummy Chocolate Brownies**

**Image gallery — over 50 images of paintings, crafts, and other photos of Jolly Good Art stud paintings by Tanya Fr**

**Web links**

**People and organizat**